Copula Modeling:
An Introduction
for Practitioners

Copula Modeling: An Introduction for Practitioners

Pravin K. Trivedi

Department of Economics, Indiana University
Wylie Hall 105
Bloomington, IN 47405
trivedi@indiana.edu

David M. Zimmer

Western Kentucky University, Department of Economics
1906 College Heights Blvd.
Bowling Green, KY 42101
dmzimmer@gmail.com
formerly at U.S. Federal Trade Commission

the essence of knowledge

Boston – Delft

Foundations and Trends® in Econometrics

Published, sold and distributed by:
now Publishers Inc.
PO Box 1024
Hanover, MA 02339
USA
Tel. +1-781-985-4510
www.nowpublishers.com
sales@nowpublishers.com

Outside North America:
now Publishers Inc.
PO Box 179
2600 AD Delft
The Netherlands
Tel. +31-6-51115274

The preferred citation for this publication is P. K. Trivedi and D. M. Zimmer, Copula Modeling: An Introduction for Practitioners, Foundations and Trends® in Econometrics, vol 1, no 1, pp 1–111, 2005

Printed on acid-free paper

ISBN: 978-1-60198-020-5
© 2007 P. K. Trivedi and D. M. Zimmer

Foundations and Trends® in Econometrics
Volume 1 Issue 1, 2005
Editorial Board

Editorial Scope

Foundations and Trends® in Econometrics will publish survey and tutorial articles in the following topics:

- Identification
- Model Choice and Specification Analysis
- Non-linear Regression Models
- Simultaneous Equation Models
- Estimation Frameworks
- Biased Estimation
- Computational Problems
- Microeconometrics
- Treatment Modeling
- Discrete Choice Modeling
- Models for Count Data
- Duration Models
- Limited Dependent Variables
- Panel Data
- Dynamic Specification
- Inference and Causality
- Continuous Time Stochastic Models

- Modeling Non-linear Time Series
- Unit Roots
- Cointegration
- Latent Variable Models
- Qualitative Response Models
- Hypothesis Testing
- Interactions-based Models
- Duration Models
- Financial Econometrics
- Measurement Error in Survey Data
- Productivity Measurement and Analysis
- Semiparametric and Nonparametric Estimation
- Bootstrap Methods
- Nonstationary Time Series
- Robust Estimation

Information for Librarians

Foundations and Trends® in Econometrics, 2005, Volume 1, 4 issues. ISSN paper version 1551-3076. ISSN online version 1551-3084. Also available as a combined paper and online subscription.

Foundations and Trends® in
Econometrics
Vol. 1, No 1 (2005) 1–111
© 2007 P. K. Trivedi and D. M. Zimmer
DOI: 10.1561/0800000005

now
the essence of knowledge

Copula Modeling: An Introduction for Practitioners[*]

Pravin K. Trivedi[1] and David M. Zimmer[2]

[1] Department of Economics, Indiana University, Wylie Hall 105,
Bloomington, IN 47405, trivedi@indiana.edu
[2] Western Kentucky University, Department of Economics, 1906 College
Heights Blvd., Bowling Green, KY 42101, dmzimmer@gmail.com formerly
at U.S. Federal Trade Commission

Abstract

This article explores the copula approach for econometric modeling of
joint parametric distributions. Although theoretical foundations of copulas are complex, this text demonstrates that practical implementation
and estimation are relatively straightforward. An attractive feature of
parametrically specified copulas is that estimation and inference are
based on standard maximum likelihood procedures, and thus copulas
can be estimated using desktop econometric software. This represents
a substantial advantage of copulas over recently proposed simulation-
based approaches to joint modeling.

[*] The authors are grateful to the Editor Bill Greene and an anonymous reviewer for helpful
comments and suggestions for improvement, but retain responsibility for the contents of
the present text.

Contents

1

Introduction

This article explores the copula approach for econometric modeling of joint parametric distributions. Econometric estimation and inference for data that are assumed to be multivariate normal distributed are highly developed, but general approaches for joint nonlinear modeling of nonnormal data are not well developed, and there is a frequent tendency to consider modeling issues on a case-by-case basis. In econometrics, nonnormal and nonlinear models arise frequently in models of discrete choice, models of event counts, models based on truncated and/or censored data, and joint models with both continuous and discrete outcomes.

Existing techniques for estimating joint distributions of nonlinear outcomes often require computationally demanding simulation-based estimation procedures. Although theoretical foundations of copulas are complex, this text demonstrates that practical implementation and estimation is relatively straightforward. An attractive feature of parametrically specified copulas is that estimation and inference are based on standard maximum likelihood procedures, and thus copulas can be estimated using desktop econometric software such as Stata, Limdep, or

SAS. This represents a substantial advantage of copulas over recently proposed simulation-based approaches to joint modeling.

Interest in copulas arises from several perspectives. First, econometricians often possess more information about marginal distributions of related variables than their joint distribution. The copula approach is a useful method for deriving joint distributions given the marginal distributions, especially when the variables are nonnormal. Second, in a bivariate context, copulas can be used to define nonparametric measures of dependence for pairs of random variables. When fairly general and/or asymmetric modes of dependence are relevant, such as those that go beyond correlation or linear association, then copulas play a special role in developing additional concepts and measures. Finally, copulas are useful extensions and generalizations of approaches for modeling joint distributions and dependence that have appeared in the literature.

According to Schweizer (1991), the theorem underlying copulas was introduced in a 1959 article by Sklar written in French; a similar article written in English followed in 1973 (Sklar, 1973). Succinctly stated, copulas are functions that connect multivariate distributions to their one-dimensional margins. If F is an m-dimensional cumulative distribution function (**cdf**) with one-dimensional margins $F_1, \ldots, F_m$, then there exists an m-dimensional copula C such that $F(y_1, \ldots, y_m) = C(F_1(y_1), \ldots, F_m(y_m))$. The case $m = 2$ has attracted special attention.

The term copula was introduced by Sklar (1959). However, the idea of copula had previously appeared in a number of texts, most notably in Hoeffding (1940, 1941) who established best possible bounds for these functions and studied measures of dependence that are invariant under strictly increasing transformations. Relationships of copulas to other work is described in Nelsen (2006).

Copulas have proved useful in a variety of modeling situations. Several of the most commonly used applications are briefly mentioned:

- Financial institutions are often concerned with whether prices of different assets exhibit dependence, particularly in the tails of the joint distributions. These models typically assume that asset prices have a multivariate normal distribution, but Ané and Kharoubi (2003) and Embrechts et al. (2002) argue that this assumption is frequently unsatisfactory because large changes are observed more frequently than predicted under the normality assumption. Value at Risk (VaR) estimated under multivariate normality may lead to underestimation of the portfolio VaR. Since deviations from normality, e.g., tail dependence in the distribution of asset prices, greatly increase computational difficulties of joint asset models, modeling based on a copula parameterized by nonnormal marginals is an attractive alternative; see Bouyé et al. (2000), Klugman and Parsa (2000).

- Actuaries are interested in annuity pricing models in which the relationship between two individuals' incidence of disease or death is jointly related (Clayton, 1978). For example, actuaries have noted the existence of a "broken heart" syndrome in which an individual's death substantially increases the probability that the person's spouse will also experience death within a fixed period of time. Joint survivals of husband/wife pairs tend to exhibit nonlinear behavior with strong tail dependence and are poorly suited for models based on normality. These models are prime candidates for copula modeling.

- Many microeconometric modeling situations have marginal distributions that cannot be easily combined into joint distributions. This frequently arises in models of discrete or limited dependent variables. For example, Munkin and Trivedi (1999) explain that bivariate distributions of discrete event counts are often restrictive and difficult to estimate. Furthermore, joint modeling is especially difficult when two related variables come from different parametric families. For example, one variable might characterize a multinomial discrete choice and another might measure an event count. As there are few, if any, parametric joint distributions based on marginals from different families, the copula approach provides a general and straightforward approach for constructing joint distributions in these situations.

- In some applications, a flexible joint distribution is part of a larger modeling problem. For example, in the linear self-selection model, an outcome variable, say income, is only observed if another event occurs, say labor force participation. The likelihood function for this model includes a joint distribution for the outcome variable and the probability that the event is observed. Usually, this distribution is assumed to be multivariate normal, but Smith (2003) demonstrates that for some applications, a flexible copula representation is more appropriate.

Several excellent monographs and surveys are already available, particularly those by Joe (1997) and Nelsen (2006). Schweizer and Sklar 1983, ch. 6, provide a mathematical account of developments on copulas over three decades. Nelsen (1991) focuses on copulas and measures of association. Other surveys take a contextual approach. Frees and Valdez (1998) provide an introduction for actuaries that summarizes statistical properties and applications and is especially helpful to new entrants to the field. Georges et al. (2001) provide a review of copula applications to multivariate survival analysis. Cherubini et al. (2004) focus on financial applications, but they also provide an excellent coverage of copula foundations for the benefit of a reader who may be new to the area. For those whose main concern is with modeling dependence using copulas, Embrechts et al. (2002) provide a lucid and thorough coverage.

In econometrics there is a relatively small literature that uses copulas in an explicit manner. Miller and Liu (2002) mention the copula method in their survey of methods of recovering joint distributions from limited information. Several texts have modeled sample selection using bivariate latent variable distributions that can be interpreted as specific examples of copula functions even though the term copula or copula properties are not explicitly used; see Lee (1983), Prieger (2002) and van Ophem (1999, 2000). However, Smith (2003) explicitly uses the (Archimedean) copula framework to analyze the self-selection problem. Similarly for the case of joint discrete distributions, a number of studies that explore models of correlated count variables, without explicitly using copulas, are developed in Cameron et al. (1988), Munkin and Trivedi (1999), and Chib and Winkelmann (2001). Cameron et al. (2004), use the copula framework to analyze the empirical distribution of two counted measures of the same event. Zimmer and Trivedi (2006) use a trivariate copula framework to analyze a selection model with counted outcomes. In financial econometrics and time series analysis, the copula approach has attracted considerable attention recently. Bouyé et al. (2000) and Cherubini et al. (2004) cover many issues and financial applications. A central issue is on the nature of dependence and hence the interpretation of a copula as a dependence function dominates. See Patton (forthcoming) for further discussion of copulas in time series settings.

The purpose of this article is to provide practitioners with a useful guide to copula modeling. Special attention is dedicated to issues related to estimation and misspecification. Although our main focus is using copulas in an applied setting, particularly cross sectional microeconometric applications, it is necessary to cover important theoretical foundations related to joint distributions, dependence, and copula generation. Sections 2 and 3 primarily deal with these theoretical issues. The reader who is already familiar with the basics of copulas and dependence may wish to skip directly to Section 4, which highlights issues of estimation and presents several empirical applications. Section 5 offers concluding remarks as well as suggestions for future research. Throughout the text, various Monte Carlo experiments and simulations are used to demonstrate copula properties. Methods for generating random numbers from copulas are presented in the Appendix.

2

Copulas and Dependence

Copulas are parametrically specified joint distributions generated from given marginals. Therefore, properties of copulas are analogous to properties of joint distributions. This Section begins by outlining several important properties and results for joint distributions that are frequently used in the context of copulas. Copulas are formally introduced in Section 2.2, followed by specific examples in Section 2.3. The important topic of characterizing and measuring dependence is covered in Section 2.4.

2.1 Basics of Joint Distributions

The joint distribution of a set of random variables $(Y_1, \ldots, Y_m)$ is defined as

$$F(y_1, \ldots, y_m) = \Pr[Y_i \leq y_i; \ i = 1, \ldots, m], \qquad (2.1)$$

and the **survival function** corresponding to $F(y_1, \ldots, y_m)$ is given by

$$\overline{F}(y_1, \ldots, y_m) = \Pr[Y_i > y_i; \ i = 1, \ldots, m]$$
$$= 1 - F(y_1) \quad \text{for } m = 1$$

$$= 1 - F_1(y_1) - F_2(y_2) + F_1(y_1)F_2(y_2) \quad \text{for } m = 2$$
$$= 1 - F_1(y_1) - F_2(y_2) - F_3(y_1) + F_{12}(y_1, y_2)$$
$$+ F_{13}(y_1, y_3) + F_{23}(y_2, y_3) - F(y_1, y_2, y_3) \quad \text{for } m = 3;$$

the last equality does not hold for the independence case.

2.1.1   Bivariate cdf properties

The following conditions are necessary and sufficient for a right-continuous function to be bivariate cdf:

(1) $\lim_{y_j \to -\infty} F(y_1, y_2) = 0$, $j = 1, 2$;
(2) $\lim_{y_j \to \infty \forall j} F(y_1, y_2) = 1$,
(3) By the **rectangle inequality**, for all (a_1, a_2) and (b_1, b_2) with $a_1 \le b_1, a_2 \le b_2$,

$$F(b_1, b_2) - F(a_1, b_2) - F(b_1, a_2) + F(a_1, a_2) \ge 0. \qquad (2.2)$$

Conditions 1 and 2 imply $0 \le F \le 1$. Condition 3 is referred to as the property that F is **2-increasing**. If F has second derivatives, then the 2-increasing property is equivalent to $\partial^2 F / \partial y_1 \partial y_2 \ge 0$.

Given the bivariate cdf $F(y_1, y_2)$:

(1) univariate margins (or marginal distribution functions) F_1 and F_2 are obtained by letting $y_2 \to \infty$ and $y_1 \to \infty$, respectively. That is, $F_1(y_1) = \lim_{y_2 \to \infty} F(y_1, y_2)$ and $F_2(y_2) = \lim_{y_1 \to \infty} F(y_1, y_2)$;
(2) the conditional distribution functions $F_{1|2}(y_1 | y_2)$ and $F_{2|1}(y_2 | y_1)$ are obtained by $\partial F(y_1, y_2) / \partial y_2$ and $\partial F(y_1, y_2) / \partial y_1$, respectively.

The multivariate cdf $F(y_1, y_2, \ldots, y_m)$ has the following properties:

(1) $\lim_{y_j \to -\infty} F(y_1, y_2, \ldots, y_m) = 0$, $j = 1, 2, \ldots, m$;
(2) $\lim_{y_j \to \infty \forall j} F(y_1, \ldots, y_m) = 1$.

The pseudo-generalized **inverse of a distribution function** is denoted $F_j^{-1}(t)$ which is defined as

$$F_j^{-1}(t) = \inf[y_j : F_j(y_j) \ge t, \, 0 < t < 1]. \qquad (2.3)$$

2.1.2 Fréchet–Hoeffding bounds

Consider any m-variate joint cdf $F(y_1,\ldots,y_m)$ with univariate marginal cdfs $F_1,\ldots,F_m$. By definition, each marginal distribution can take any value in the range $[0,1]$. The joint cdf is bounded below and above by the Fréchet–Hoeffding lower and upper bounds, F_L and F_U, defined as

$$F_L(y_1,\ldots,y_m) = \max\left[\sum_{j=1}^{m} F_j - m + 1, 0\right] = W,$$

$$F_U(y_1,\ldots,y_m) = \min[F_1,\ldots,F_m] = M,$$

so that

$$W = \max\left[\sum_{j=1}^{m} F_j - m + 1, 0\right] \leq F(y_1,\ldots,y_m) \leq \min[F_1,\ldots,F_m] = M,$$

(2.4)

where the upper bound is always a cdf, and the lower bound is a cdf for $m = 2$. For $m > 2$, F_L may be a cdf under some conditions (see Theorem 3.6 in Joe, 1997).

In the case of univariate margins, the term Fréchet–Hoeffding class refers to the class of m-variate distributions $\mathcal{F}(F_1, F_2,\ldots, F_m)$ in which margins are fixed or given. In the case where the margins are bivariate or higher dimensional, the term refers to the classes such as $\mathcal{F}(F_{12}, F_{13})$, $\mathcal{F}(F_{12}, F_{13}, F_{23})$.

2.2 Copula Functions

Unless stated otherwise the discussion in this section is limited to the case of one-dimensional margins. We begin with the definition of copula, following Schweizer (1991).

2.2.1 Sklar's theorem

Sklar's Theorem states that an m-dimensional copula (or m-copula) is a function C from the unit m-cube $[0,1]^m$ to the unit interval $[0,1]$ which satisfies the following conditions:

(1) $C(1,\ldots,1,a_n,1,\ldots,1) = a_n$ for every $n \leq m$ and all a_n in $[0,1]$;

(2) $C(a_1, \ldots, a_m) = 0$ if $a_n = 0$ for any $n \leq m$;

(3) C is m-increasing.

Property 1 says that if the realizations of $m - 1$ variables are known each with marginal probability one, then the joint probability of the m outcomes is the same as the probability of the remaining uncertain outcome. Property 2 is sometimes referred to as the **grounded** property of a copula. It says that the joint probability of all outcomes is zero if the marginal probability of any outcome is zero. Property 3 says that the C-volume of any m-dimensional interval is non-negative. Properties 2 and 3 are general properties of multivariate cdfs that were previously mentioned.

It follows that an m-copula can be defined as an m-dimensional cdf whose support is contained in $[0,1]^m$ and whose one-dimensional margins are uniform on $[0,1]$. In other words, an m-copula is an m-dimensional distribution function with all m univariate margins being $U(0,1)$. To see the relationship between distribution functions and copulas, consider a continuous m-variate distribution function $F(y_1, \ldots, y_m)$ with univariate marginal distributions $F_1(y_1), \ldots, F_m(y_m)$ and inverse (quantile) functions $F_1^{-1}, \ldots, F_m^{-1}$. Then $y_1 = F_1^{-1}(u_1) \sim F_1, \ldots, y_m = F_m^{-1}(u_m) \sim F_m$ where $u_1, \ldots, u_m$ are uniformly distributed variates. The transforms of uniform variates are distributed as F_i ($i = 1, \ldots, m$). Hence

$$\begin{aligned}
F(y_1, \ldots, y_m) &= F(F_1^{-1}(u_1), \ldots, F_m^{-1}(u_m)) \\
&= \Pr[U_1 \leq u_1, \ldots, U_m \leq u_m] \\
&= C(u_1, \ldots, u_m)
\end{aligned} \tag{2.5}$$

is the unique copula associated with the distribution function. That is if $y \sim F$, and F is continuous then

$$(F_1(y_1), \ldots, F_m(y_m)) \sim C,$$

and if $\mathbf{U} \sim C$, then

$$(F_1^{-1}(u_1), \ldots, F_m^{-1}(u_m)) \sim F.$$

2.2.2   Practical implications of Sklar's theorem

The above results imply that copulas can be used to express a multivariate distribution in terms of its marginal distributions. Econometricians often know a great deal about marginal distributions of individual variables but little about their joint behavior. Copulas allow researchers to piece together joint distributions when only marginal distributions are known with certainty. For an m-variate function F, the copula associated with F is a distribution function $C : [0,1]^m \rightarrow [0,1]$ that satisfies

$$F(y_1, \ldots, y_m) = C(F_1(y_1), \ldots, F_m(y_m); \theta), \qquad (2.6)$$

where θ is a parameter of the copula called the **dependence parameter**, which measures dependence between the marginals.

Equation (2.6) is a frequent starting point of empirical applications of copulas. Although θ may be a vector of parameters, for bivariate applications it is customary to specify it as a scalar measure of dependence. Thus, the joint distribution is expressed in terms of its respective marginal distributions and a function C that binds them together. A substantial advantage of copula functions is that the marginal distributions may come from different families. This construction allows researchers to consider marginal distributions and dependence as two separate but related issues. For many empirical applications, the dependence parameter is the main focus of estimation. Note that because copulas are multivariate distributions of $U(0,1)$ variables, copulas are expressed in terms of marginal probabilities (cdfs).

If the margins $F_1(Y_1), \ldots, F_m(Y_m)$ are continuous, then the corresponding copula in Eq. (2.6) is unique, and otherwise it is uniquely determined. The latter statement means that the uniqueness property only holds on $\text{Ran}(F_1) \times \text{Ran}(F_2) \times \cdots \times \text{Ran}(F_m)$. The result can be applied to the case of discrete margins and/or mixed continuous and discrete margins. If $F_1, \ldots, F_m$ are not all continuous, the joint distribution function can always be expressed as (2.6), although in such a case the copula is not unique (see Schweizer and Sklar, 1983, ch. 6). In view of (2.6) and the uniqueness property of the copula, it is often viewed as a **dependence function**.

If F is discrete, then there exists a unique copula representation for F for $(u_1, \ldots, u_m) \in \text{Ran}(F_1) \times \text{Ran}(F_2) \times \cdots \times \text{Ran}(F_m)$. However, the general lack of uniqueness of a copula representation for discrete distributions is a theoretical issue which needs to be confronted in analytical proofs but does not inhibit empirical applications. Finding a unique copula for a joint distribution requires one to know the form of the joint distribution. Researchers use copulas because they do not know the form of the joint distribution, so whether working with continuous or discrete data, a pivotal modeling problem is to choose a copula that adequately captures dependence structures of the data without sacrificing attractive properties of the marginals.

To summarize: the copula approach involves specifying marginal distributions of each random variable along with a function (copula) that binds them together. The copula function can be parameterized to include measures of dependence between the marginal distributions. If the copula is a product of two marginals, then independence is obtained, and separate estimation of each marginal is appropriate. Under dependence, efficient estimation of the joint distribution, by way of a copula, is feasible. Since a copula can capture dependence structures regardless of the form of the margins, a copula approach to modeling related variables is potentially very useful to econometricians.

2.2.3   Additional properties and survival copulas

Because copulas are multivariate distribution functions, the previously-mentioned Frèchet–Hoeffding bounds also apply to copulas; that is,

$$W = \max \left[\sum_{j=1}^{m} F_j - m + 1, 0 \right] \leq C(y_1, \ldots, y_m) \leq \min[F_1, \ldots, F_m] = M.$$

(2.7)

Note that the upper bound is itself a distribution function and hence a copula. So we denote the upper bound as $C_U(y_1, \ldots, y_m)$. If the lower bound is also a copula, then it is denoted as $C_L(y_1, \ldots, y_m)$. This leads to the Frèchet–Hoeffding bounds for copulas:

$$C_L(y_1, \ldots, y_m) \leq C(y_1, \ldots, y_m) \leq C_U(y_1, \ldots, y_m). \qquad (2.8)$$

Knowledge of Frèchet–Hoeffding bounds is important in selecting an appropriate copula. A desirable feature of a copula is that it should cover the sample space between the lower and the upper bounds and that as θ approaches the lower (upper) bound of its permissible range, the copula approaches the Frèchet–Hoeffding lower (upper) bound.

However, the parametric form of a copula may impose restrictions such that the full coverage between the bounds is not attained and that one or both Fréchet–Hoeffding bounds are not included in the permissible range. Therefore, a particular copula may be a better choice for one data set than for another.

A special case of the copula – the product copula, denoted $C^\perp$, – results if the margins are independent. A family of copulas that includes $C_L, C^\perp$, and C_U, is said to be comprehensive.

Several additional properties of copulas deserve mention due to their attractive implications for empirical applications; it is convenient to state these for the case $m = 2$. First, Y_1 and Y_2 are **independent** iff C is a product copula, i.e., $C(y_1, y_2) = F_1(y_1)F_2(y_2)$. In contrast, perfect positive or negative dependence is defined in terms of **comonotonicity** or **countermonotonicity**, respectively. For any (y_{1j}, y_{2j}), (y_{1k}, y_{2k}) a comonotonic set is that for which $\{y_{1j} \leq y_{2j}, y_{1k} \leq y_{2k}\}$ or $\{y_{1j} \geq y_{2j}, y_{1k} \geq y_{2k}\}$. The set is said to be countermonotonic if $\{y_{1j} \leq y_{2j}, y_{1k} \geq y_{2k}\}$ or $\{y_{1j} \leq y_{2j}, y_{1k} \geq y_{2k}\}$. Second, Y_1 is an increasing function of Y_2 iff $C(\cdot) = C_U(\cdot)$, which corresponds to comonotonicity and perfect positive dependence. Third, Y_1 is a decreasing function of Y_2 iff $C(\cdot) = C_L(\cdot)$, which corresponds to countermonotonicity and perfect negative dependence. That is, the association is positive if the copula attains the upper Fréchet–Hoeffding bound and negative if it attains the lower Fréchet–Hoeffding bound. Fourth, copulas have an attractive **invariance property** by which the dependence captured by a copula is invariant with respect to increasing and continuous transformations of the marginal distributions; see Schweizer and Sklar (1983). This means that the same copula may be used for, say, the joint distribution of (Y_1, Y_2) as $(\ln Y_1, \ln Y_2)$, and thus whether the marginals are expressed in terms of natural units or logarithmic values does not affect the copula. The properties of comonotonicity and invariance jointly make copulas a useful tool in applied work.

If $(U_1, U_2) \sim C$, then there are also copulas associated with bivariate uniform pairs $(1 - U_1, 1 - U_2)$, $(U_1, 1 - U_2)$, $(1 - U_1, U_2)$. These are called **associated copulas**. Of these the first pair is of special interest because it leads to **survival copulas**. If $F_1^{-1}(u_1) \sim F_1$, then

$F_1^{-1}(1 - u_1) \sim \overline{F}_1$, and $F_2^{-1}(1 - u_2) \sim \overline{F}_2$, and hence $(1 - U_1, 1 - U_2) \sim \overline{C}$. In general

$$\begin{aligned}
\overline{F}(\mathbf{u}) &= \overline{F}(F_1^{-1}(1 - u_1), \dots, F_m^{-1}(1 - u_m)) \\
&= \overline{F}(\overline{F}_1^{-1}(u_1), \dots, \overline{F}_m^{-1}(u_m)) \\
&= \overline{C}(u_1, \dots, u_m).
\end{aligned} \tag{2.9}$$

An example where working with survival copulas is both more convenient and natural comes from actuarial studies (usually referred to as duration analysis in econometrics and lifetime data analysis in biostatistics). Consider two possibly dependent life times, denoted T_1 and T_2. Then, for $m = 2$, the joint distribution function of survival times is defined as the probability of the joint event $(T_1 \le t_1, T_2 \le t_1)$ and is given by

$$\begin{aligned}
F(t_1, t_2) &= \Pr[T_1 \le t_1, T_2 \le t_2], \\
&= 1 - \Pr[T_1 > t_1] - \Pr[T_2 > t_2] + \Pr[T_1 > t_1, T_2 > t_2].
\end{aligned}$$

The joint survival probability that $(T_1 > t_1, T_2 > t_2)$ is

$$\begin{aligned}
S(t_1, t_2) &= \Pr[T_1 > t_1, T_2 > t_2], \\
&= 1 - F(t_1) - F(t_2) + F(t_1, t_2), \\
&= S_1(t_1) + S_2(t_2) - 1 + \overline{C}(1 - S_1(t_1), 1 - S_2(t_1)), \quad (2.10)
\end{aligned}$$

where $\overline{C}(\cdot)$ is called the **survival copula**. Notice that $S(t_1, t_2)$ is now a function of the marginal survival functions only; $S_1(t_1)$ is the marginal survival probability. Given the marginal survival distributions and the copula C, the joint survival distribution can be obtained. The symmetry property of copulas allows one to work with copulas or survival copulas (Nelsen, 2006). In the more general notation for univariate random variables Eq. (2.10) can be written as

$$\overline{C}(u_1, u_2) = u_1 + u_2 - 1 + C(1 - u_1, 1 - u_2) = \Pr[U_1 > u_1, U_2 > u_2].$$

2.3 Some Common Bivariate Copulas

Once a researcher has specified the marginal distributions, an appropriate copula is selected. Because copulas separate marginal distributions from dependence structures, the appropriate copula for a particular application is the one which best captures dependence features of the data. A large number of copulas have been proposed in the literature, and each of these imposes a different dependence structure on the data. Hutchinson and Lai (1990), Joe (1997, ch. 5), and Nelsen (2006: 116–119) provide a thorough coverage of bivariate copulas and their properties. In this section, we discuss several copulas that have appeared frequently in empirical applications, and we briefly explain dependence structures of each copula. A more detailed discussion of dependence is given in Section 2.4, and graphical illustrations of dependence are provided in Section 2.5. Here we write copulas in terms of random variables U_1 and U_2 that have standard uniform marginal distributions. Table 2.1 summarizes several bivariate copula functions.

2.3.1 Product copula

The simplest copula, the product copula, has the form

$$C(u_1, u_2) = u_1 u_2, \tag{2.11}$$

where u_1 and u_2 take values in the unit interval of the real line. The product copula is important as a benchmark because it corresponds to independence.

2.3.2 Farlie–Gumbel–Morgenstern copula

The Farlie–Gumbel–Morgenstern (FGM) copula takes the form

$$C(u_1, u_2; \theta) = u_1 u_2 \left(1 + \theta(1 - u_1)(1 - u_2)\right). \tag{2.12}$$

The FGM copula was first proposed by Morgenstern (1956). The FGM copula is a perturbation of the product copula; if the dependence parameter θ equals zero, then the FGM copula collapses to independence. It is attractive due to its simplicity, and Prieger (2002) advocates its use in modeling selection into health insurance plans. However, it is restrictive because this copula is only useful when dependence between the two marginals is modest in magnitude.

Table 2.1 Some standard copula functions.

Copula type	Function $C(u_1, u_2)$	θ-domain	Kendall's τ	Spearman's ρ
Product	$u_1 u_2$	N.A.	0	0
FGM	$u_1 u_2(1 + \theta(1 - u_1)(1 - u_2))$	$-1 \leq \theta \leq +1$	$\frac{2}{9}\theta$	$\frac{1}{3}\theta$
Gaussian	$\Phi_G[\Phi^{-1}(u_1), \Phi^{-1}(u_2); \theta]$	$-1 < \theta < +1$	$\frac{2}{\pi}\arcsin(\theta)$	$\frac{6}{\pi}\arcsin(\frac{\theta}{2})$
Clayton	$(u_1^{-\theta} + u_2^{-\theta} - 1)^{-1/\theta}$	$\theta \in (0, \infty)$	$\frac{\theta}{\theta+2}$	$*$
Frank	$-\frac{1}{\theta}\log\left(1 + \dfrac{(e^{-\theta u_1} - 1)(e^{-\theta u_2} - 1)}{e^{-\theta} - 1}\right)$	$\theta \in (-\infty, \infty)$	$1 - \frac{4}{\theta}[1 - D_1(\theta)]$	$1 - \frac{12}{\theta}[D_1(\theta) - D_2(\theta)]$
Ali-Mikhail-Haq	$u_1 u_2[1 - \theta(1 - u_1)(1 - u_2)]^{-1}$	$-1 \leq \theta \leq 1$	$(\frac{3\theta-2}{\theta}) \\ -\frac{2}{3}(1 - \frac{1}{\theta})^2 \ln(1 - \theta)$	$*$

Note: FGM is the Farlie–Gumbel–Morgenstern copula. The asterisk entry indicates that the expression is complicated. Notation $D_k(x)$ denotes the "Debye" function $k/x^k \int_0^x \frac{t^k}{(e^t - 1)} dt$, $k = 1, 2$.

2.3.3   Gaussian (Normal) copula

The normal copula takes the form

$$C(u_1, u_2; \theta) = \Phi_G \left(\Phi^{-1}(u_1), \Phi^{-1}(u_2); \theta \right),$$

$$= \int_{-\infty}^{\Phi^{-1}(u_1)} \int_{-\infty}^{\Phi^{-1}(u_2)} \frac{1}{2\pi(1 - \theta^2)^{1/2}}$$

$$\times \left\{ \frac{-(s^2 - 2\theta st + t^2)}{2(1 - \theta^2)} \right\} ds dt \qquad (2.13)$$

where Φ is the cdf of the standard normal distribution, and $\Phi_G(u_1, u_2)$ is the standard bivariate normal distribution with correlation parameter θ restricted to the interval $(-1, 1)$. This is the copula function proposed by Lee (1983) for modeling selectivity in the context of continuous but nonnormal distributions. The idea was exploited by others without making an explicit connection with copulas. For example, Van Ophem (1999) used it to analyze dependence in a bivariate count model. As the dependence parameter approaches -1 and 1, the normal copula attains the Fréchet lower and upper bound, respectively. The normal copula is flexible in that it allows for equal degrees of positive and negative dependence and includes both Fréchet bounds in its permissible range.

2.3.4   Student's *t*-copula

An example of a copula with two dependence parameters is that for the bivariate *t*-distribution with ν degrees of freedom and correlation ρ,

$$C^t(u_1, u_2; \theta_1, \theta_2) = \int_{-\infty}^{t_{\theta_1}^{-1}(u_1)} \int_{-\infty}^{t_{\theta_2}^{-1}(u_2)} \frac{1}{2\pi(1 - \theta_2^2)^{1/2}}$$

$$\times \left\{ 1 + \frac{(s^2 - 2\theta_2 st + t^2)}{\nu(1 - \theta_2^2)} \right\}^{-(\theta_1 + 2)/2} ds dt, \qquad (2.14)$$

where $t_{\theta_1}^{-1}(u_1)$ denotes the inverse of the cdf of the standard univariate *t*-distribution with θ_1 degrees of freedom. The two dependence parameters are (θ_1, θ_2). The parameter θ_1 controls the heaviness of the tails. For $\theta_1 < 3$, the variance does not exist and for $\theta_1 < 5$, the fourth moment does not exist. As $\theta_1 \to \infty$, $C^t(u_1, u_2; \theta_1, \theta_2) \to \Phi_G(u_1, u_2; \theta_2)$.

2.3.5   Clayton copula

The Clayton (1978) copula, also referred to as the Cook and Johnson (1981) copula, originally studied by Kimeldorf and Sampson (1975), takes the form:

$$C(u_1, u_2; \theta) = (u_1^{-\theta} + u_2^{-\theta} - 1)^{-1/\theta} \qquad (2.15)$$

with the dependence parameter θ restricted on the region $(0, \infty)$. As θ approaches zero, the marginals become independent. As θ approaches infinity, the copula attains the Fréchet upper bound, but for no value does it attain the Fréchet lower bound. The Clayton copula cannot account for negative dependence. It has been used to study correlated risks because it exhibits strong left tail dependence and relatively weak right tail dependence. Anecdotal and empirical evidence suggests that loan defaults are highly correlated during recessionary times. Similarly, researchers have studied the "broken heart syndrome" in which spouses' ages at death tend to be correlated. When correlation between two events, such as performance of two funds or spouses' ages at death, is strongest in the left tail of the joint distribution, Clayton is an appropriate modeling choice.

2.3.6   Frank copula

The Frank copula (1979) takes the form:

$$C(u_1, u_2; \theta) = -\theta^{-1} \log \left\{ 1 + \frac{(e^{-\theta u_1} - 1)(e^{-\theta u_2} - 1)}{e^{-\theta} - 1} \right\}.$$

The dependence parameter may assume any real value $(-\infty, \infty)$. Values of $-\infty$, 0, and ∞ correspond to the Fréchet lower bound, independence, and Fréchet upper bound, respectively. The Frank copula is popular for several reasons. First, unlike some other copulas, it permits negative dependence between the marginals. Second, dependence is symmetric in both tails, similar to the Gaussian and Student-t copulas. Third, it is "comprehensive" in the sense that both Fréchet bounds are included in the range of permissible dependence. Consequently, the Frank copula can, in theory, be used to model outcomes with strong positive or negative dependence. However, as simulations reported below illustrate, dependence in the tails of the Frank copula tends to be relatively weak compared to the Gaussian copula, and the strongest dependence is centered in the middle of the distribution, which suggests that the Frank copula is most appropriate for data that exhibit weak tail dependence. This copula has been widely used in empirical applications (Meester and MacKay, 1994).

2.3.7 Gumbel copula

The Gumbel copula (1960) takes the form:

$$C(u_1, u_2; \theta) = \exp\left(-(\tilde{u}_1^\theta + \tilde{u}_2^\theta)^{1/\theta}\right),$$

where $\tilde{u}_j = -\log u_j$. The dependence parameter is restricted to the interval $[1, \infty)$. Values of 1 and ∞ correspond to independence and the Fréchet upper bound, but this copula does not attain the Fréchet lower bound for any value of θ. Similar to the Clayton copula, Gumbel does not allow negative dependence, but it contrast to Clayton, Gumbel exhibits strong right tail dependence and relatively weak left tail dependence. If outcomes are known to be strongly correlated at high values but less correlated at low values, then the Gumbel copula is an appropriate choice.

2.4 Measuring Dependence

Given a bewilderingly wide range of copulas, how should one choose between them in empirical work? What is the nature of dependence that is captured by the dependence parameter(s) in different copulas? How does the dependence parameter relate to the more familiar concept of correlation? These issues, as well as those of computational convenience and interpretability, are relevant to the choice among different copulas. A key consideration is the ability of a model to capture the dependence between variables in a contextually satisfactory manner. A proper discussion of this issue requires discussion of dependence in greater detail; see, for example, Drouet-Mari and Kotz (2001).

In this section, we restrict the discussion to the bivariate case although generalization to higher dimensions is possible. Further, we

denote this pair as (X,Y) rather than (Y_1,Y_2) in order to ensure nota-
tional consistency with statistical literature on dependence.

2.4.1   Desirable properties of dependence measures

The random variables (X,Y) are said to be dependent or associated
if they are not independent in the sense that $F(X,Y) \neq F_1(X)F_2(Y)$.
In the bivariate case let $\delta(X,Y)$ denote a scalar measure of dependence. Embrechts et al. (2002) list four desirable properties of this
measure:

(1) $\delta(X,Y) = \delta(Y,X)$ (symmetry);
(2) $-1 \leq \delta(X,Y) \leq +1$ (normalization);
(3) $\delta(X,Y) = 1 \Leftrightarrow (X,Y)$ comonotonic; $\delta(X,Y) = -1 \Leftrightarrow (X,Y)$
      countermonotonic;
(4) For a strictly monotonic transformation $T : \mathcal{R} \to \mathcal{R}$ of X :

$$\delta(T(X),Y) = \begin{cases} \delta(Y,X)T \text{ increasing} \\ -\delta(Y,X)T \text{ decreasing.} \end{cases}$$

Cherubini et al. (2004: 95) note that association can be measured
using several alternative concepts and examine four in particular: linear correlation; concordance; tail dependence; and positive quadrant
dependence. We shall consider these in turn.

2.4.2   Correlation and dependence

By far the most familiar association (dependence) concept is the **correlation coefficient** between a pair of variables (X,Y), defined as

$$\rho_{XY} = \frac{\text{cov}[X,Y]}{\sigma_X \sigma_Y},$$

where $\text{cov}[X,Y] = E[XY] - E[X]E[Y]$, $\sigma_X, \sigma_Y > 0$, σ_X and σ_Y denote
the standard deviations of X and Y, respectively. This measure of
association can be extended to the multivariate case $m \geq 3$, for which
the covariance and correlation measures are symmetric positive definite
matrices.

It is well known that: (a) ρ_{XY} is a measure of **linear dependence**, (b) ρ_{XY} is **symmetric**, and (c) that the lower and

upper bounds on the inequality $-1 < \rho_{XY} < 1$ measure perfect negative and positive linear dependence (a property referred to as **normalization**), and (d) it is invariant with respect to linear transformations of the variables. Further, if the pair (X, Y) follows a bivariate normal distribution, then the correlation is fully informative about their joint dependence, and $\rho_{XY} = 0$ implies and is implied by independence. In this case, the dependence structure (copula) is fully determined by the correlation, and zero correlation and independence are equivalent.

In the case of other multivariate distributions, such as the **multivariate elliptical families** that share some properties of the multivariate normal, the dependence structure is also fully determined by the correlation matrix; see Fang and Zhang (1990). However, in general zero correlation does not imply independence. For example, if $X \sim \mathcal{N}(0,1)$, and $Y = X^2$, then $\mathrm{cov}[X, Y] = 0$, but (X, Y) are clearly dependent. Zero correlation only requires $\mathrm{cov}[X, Y] = 0$, whereas zero dependence requires $\mathrm{cov}[\phi_1(X), \phi_2(Y)] = 0$ for any functions ϕ_1 and ϕ_2. This represents a weakness of correlation as a measure of dependence. A second limitation of correlation is that it is not defined for some heavy-tailed distributions whose second moments do not exist, e.g., some members of the stable class and Student's t distribution with degrees of freedom equal to 2 or 1. Many financial time series display the distributional property of heavy tails and nonexistence of higher moments; see, for example, Cont (2001). Boyer et al. (1999) found that correlation measures were not sufficiently informative in the presence of asymmetric dependence. A third limitation of the correlation measure is that it is not invariant under strictly increasing nonlinear transformations. That is $\rho[T(X), T(Y)] \neq \rho_{XY}$ for $T : \mathcal{R} \to \mathcal{R}$. Given these limitations, alternative measures of dependence should be considered. Finally, attainable values of the correlation coefficient within the interval $[-1, +1]$ between a pair of variables depend upon their respective marginal distributions F_1 and F_2 which place bounds on the value. These limitations motivate an alternative measure of dependence, rank correlation, which we consider in the next section.

2.4.3   Rank correlation

Consider two random variables X and Y with continuous distribution functions F_1 and F_2, respectively, and joint distribution function F. Two well-established measures of correlation are Spearman's rank correlation ("Spearman's rho"), defined as

$$\rho_S(X,Y) = \rho(F_1(X), F_2(Y)), \qquad (2.16)$$

and Kendall's rank correlation ("Kendall's tau") defined as

$$\rho_\tau(X,Y) = \Pr[(X_1 - X_2)(Y_1 - Y_2) > 0] - \Pr[(X_1 - X_2)(Y_1 - Y_2) < 0], \qquad (2.17)$$

where (X_1, Y_1) and (X_2, Y_2) are two independent pairs of random variables from F. The first term on the right, $\Pr[(X_1 - X_2)(Y_1 - Y_2) > 0]$, is referred to as $\Pr[\text{concordance}]$, the second as $\Pr[\text{discordance}]$, and hence

$$\rho_\tau(X,Y) = \Pr[\text{concordance}] - \Pr[\text{discordance}] \qquad (2.18)$$

is a measure of the relative difference between the two.

Spearman's rho is the linear correlation between $F_1(X)$ and $F_2(Y)$, which are integral transforms of X and Y. In this sense it is a measure of rank correlation. Both $\rho_S(X,Y)$ and $\rho_\tau(X,Y)$ are measures of monotonic dependence between (X,Y). Both measures are based on the concept of **concordance**, which refers to the property that large values of one random variable are associated with large values of another, whereas discordance refers to large values of one being associated with small values of the other.

The following properties of $\rho_S(X,Y)$ and $\rho_\tau(X,Y)$ are stated and proved by Embrechts et al. (2002; Theorem 3):

Both $\rho_S(X,Y)$ and $\rho_\tau(X,Y)$ have the property of symmetry, normalization, co- and countermonotonicity, and assume the value zero under independence. Further,

$$\rho_S(X,Y) = \rho_\tau(X,Y) = -1 \quad \text{iff } C = C_L,$$
$$\rho_S(X,Y) = \rho_\tau(X,Y) = 1 \quad \text{iff } C = C_U.$$

Both $\rho_S(X,Y)$ and $\rho_\tau(X,Y)$ can be expressed in terms of copulas as follows:

$$\rho_S(X,Y) = 12 \int_0^1 \int_0^1 \{C(u_1, u_2) - u_1 u_2\} \, du_1 du_2, \qquad (2.19)$$

$$\rho_\tau(X,Y) = 4 \int_0^1 \int_0^1 C(u_1, u_2) \, dC(u_1, u_2) - 1 \qquad (2.20)$$

see Joe (1997) or Schweizer and Wolff (1981) for details. There are other equivalent expressions for these measures. For example, (2.19) can be expressed as $\rho_S = 3 \int_0^1 \int_0^1 [u_1 + u_2 - 1]^2 - [u_1 - u_2]^2 dC(u_1 u_2)$; see Nelsen (2006: 185). It is also possible to obtain bounds on $\rho_S(X,Y)$ in terms of $\rho_\tau(X,Y)$, see Cherubini et al. (2004, p. 103). Also $\rho_S(X,Y) = \rho_\tau(X,Y) = 1$ iff $C = C_U$ iff $Y = T(X)$ with T increasing; and $\rho_S(X,Y) = \rho_\tau(X,Y) = -1$ iff $C = C_L$ iff $Y = T(X)$ with T decreasing.

Although the rank correlation measures have the property of invariance under monotonic transformations and can capture perfect dependence, they are not simple functions of moments and hence computation is more involved; see some examples in Table 2.1. In some cases one can use (2.19) or (2.20).

The relationship between ρ_τ and ρ_S is shown by a pair of inequalities due to Durbin and Stuart (1951) who showed that

$$\frac{3}{2}\rho_\tau - \frac{1}{2} \leq \rho_s \leq \frac{1}{2} + \rho_\tau - \frac{1}{2}\rho_\tau^2 \quad \text{for } \rho_\tau \geq 0,$$

$$\frac{1}{2}\rho_\tau^2 + \rho_\tau - \frac{1}{2} \leq \rho_s \leq \frac{3}{2}\rho_\tau + \frac{1}{2} \quad \text{for } \rho_\tau \leq 0.$$

These inequalities form the basis of a widely presented 4-quadrant diagram that displays the (ρ_s, ρ_τ)-region; see Figure 2.1. Nelsen (1991) presents expressions for ρ_S and ρ_τ and their relationship for a number of copula families. He shows that "...While the difference between ρ [ρ_S] and τ [ρ_τ] can be as much as 0.5 for some copulas, ...for many of these families, there is nearly a functional relationship between the two."

For continuous copulas, some researchers convert the dependence parameter of the copula function to a measure such as Kendall's tau or Spearman's rho which are both bounded on the interval $[-1, 1]$,

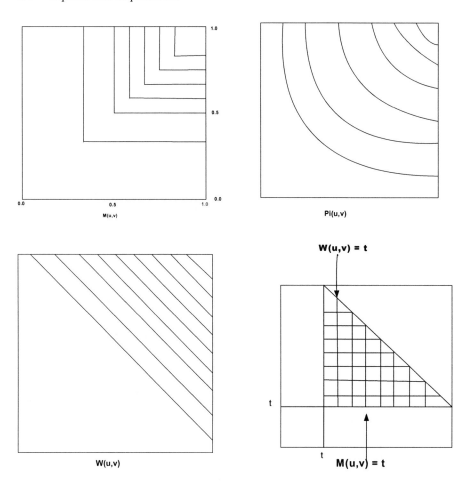

Fig. 2.1 Clockwise: upper bound; independence copula; level sets; lower bound.

and they do not depend on the functional forms of the marginal distributions.

Dependence Measures for Discrete Data. Dependence measures for continuous data do not, in general, apply directly to discrete data. Concordance measures for bivariate discrete data are subject to constraints (Marshall, 1996, Denuit and Lambert, 2005). Reconsider (2.17) in the context of discrete variables. Unlike the case of continuous random variables, the discrete case has to allow for ties, i.e.,

$\Pr[\text{tie}] = \Pr[X_1 = X_2 \text{ or } Y_1 = Y_2]$. Some attractive properties of ρ_τ for continuous variables are consequently lost in the discrete case. Several modified versions of ρ_τ and other dependence measures exist that handle the ties in different ways; see Denuit and Lambert (2005) for discussion and additional references. When (X,Y) are nonnegative integers,

$$\Pr[\text{concordance}] - \Pr[\text{discordance}] + \Pr[\text{tie}] = 1,$$

so

$$\begin{aligned}
\rho_\tau(X,Y) &= 2\Pr[\text{concordance}] - 1 + \Pr[\text{tie}], \\
&= 4\Pr[X_2 < X_1, Y_2 < Y_1] - 1 + \Pr[X_1 = X_2 \text{ or } Y_1 = Y_2].
\end{aligned}$$
$$(2.21)$$

This analysis shows that in the discrete case $\rho_\tau(X,Y)$ does depend on the margins. Also it is reduced in magnitude by the presence of ties. When the number of distinct realized values of (X,Y) is small, there is likely to be a higher proportion of ties and the attainable value of $\rho_\tau(X,Y)$ will be smaller. Denuit and Lambert (2005) obtain an upper bound and show, for example, that in the bivariate case with identical $Poisson(\mu)$ margins, the upper bound for $\rho_\tau(X,Y)$ increases monotonically with μ.

2.4.4 Tail dependence

In some cases the concordance between extreme (tail) values of random variables is of interest. For example, one may be interested in the probability that stock indexes in two countries exceed (or fall below) given levels. This requires a dependence measure for upper and lower tails of the distribution. Such a dependence measure is essentially related to the conditional probability that one index exceeds some value given that another exceeds some value. If such a conditional probability measure is a function of the copula, then it too will be invariant under strictly increasing transformations.

The tail dependence measure can be defined in terms of the joint survival function $S(u_1, u_2)$ for standard uniform random variables u_1 and u_2. Specifically, λ_L and λ_U are measures of lower and upper tail dependence, respectively, defined by

$$\lambda_L = \lim_{v \to 0^+} \frac{C(v,v)}{v}, \tag{2.22}$$

$$\lambda_U = \lim_{v \to 1^-} \frac{S(v,v)}{1-v}. \tag{2.23}$$

The expression $S(v,v) = \Pr[U_1 > v, U_2 > v]$ represents the joint survival function where $U_1 = F_1^{-1}(X), U_2 = F_2^{-1}(Y)$. The upper tail dependence measure λ_U is the limiting value of $S(v,v)/(1-v)$, which is the conditional probability $\Pr[U_1 > v | U_2 > v]$ $(= \Pr[U_2 > v | U_1 > v])$; the lower tail dependence measure λ_L is the limiting value of the conditional probability $C(v,v)/v$, which is the conditional probability $\Pr[U_1 < v | U_2 < v]$ $(= \Pr[U_2 < v | U_1 < v])$. The measure λ_U is widely used in actuarial applications of extreme value theory to handle the probability that one event is extreme conditional on another extreme event.

Two other properties related to tail dependence are left tail decreasing (LTD) and right tail increasing (RTI). Y is said to be LTD in x if $\Pr[Y \leq y | X \leq x]$ is decreasing in x for all y. Y is said to be RTI in X if $\Pr[Y > y | X > x]$ is increasing in x for all y. A third conditional probability of interest is $\Pr[Y > y | X = x]$. Y is said to be stochastically increasing if this probability is increasing in x for all y.

For copulas with simple analytical expressions, the computation of λ_U can be straight-forward, being a simple function of the dependence parameter. For example, for the Gumbel copula λ_U equals $2 - 2^\theta$. In cases where the copula's analytical expression is not available, Embrechts et al. (2002) suggest using the conditional probability representation. They also point out interesting properties of some standard copulas. For example, the bivariate Gaussian copula has the property of asymptotic independence. They remark: "Regardless of how high a correlation we choose, if we go far enough into the tail, extreme events appear to occur independently in each margin." In contrast, the bivariate t-distribution displays asymptotic upper tail dependence even for negative and zero correlations, with dependence rising as the degrees-of-freedom parameter decreases and the marginal distributions become heavy-tailed; see Table 2.1 in Embrechts et al. (2002).

2.4.5 Positive quadrant dependence

Another measure of dependence is positive quadrant dependence (**PQD**). Two random variables X, Y are said to exhibit PQD if their copula is greater than their product, i.e., $C(u_1, u_2) > u_1 u_2$ or, simply $C \succ C^\perp$, where $C^\perp$ denotes the product copula. In terms of distribution functions PQD implies $F(x, y) \geq F_1(x)F_2(y)$ for all (x, y) in $\mathbb{R}^2$. Suppose x and y denote two financial losses or gains. The PQD property implies that the probability that losses exceed some specified values is greater when (x, y) is a dependent pair than when the two are independent for all x and y. Positive quadrant dependence implies nonnegative correlation and nonnegative rank correlation. But all these properties are implied by comonotonicity which is the strongest type of positive dependence. Note that the LTD and RTI properties imply the property of PQD.

2.5 Visual Illustration of Dependence

One way of visualizing copulas is to present contour diagrams with graphs of level sets defined as the sets in $\mathbf{I}^2$ given by $C(u, v) = $ a constant, for selected constants; see graphs shown in Figure 2.1, taken from Nelsen (2006), which show **level curves** for the upper and lower bounds and the product copula. The constant is given by the boundary condition $C(1, t) = t$. The hatched triangle in the lower right quadrant gives the copula level set $\{(u, v) \in \mathbf{I}^2 \mid C(u, v) = t\}$ whose boundaries are determined by the copula lower and upper bounds, $W(u, v)$ and $M(u, v)$, respectively. Equivalently, the information can be presented in 3-dimensions.

Unfortunately, this is not always a helpful way of visualizing the data patterns implied by different copulas. If the intention is to highlight quadrant or tail dependence, the level curves are not helpful because they may "look" similar even when the copulas have different properties. One alternative is to present two-way scatter diagrams of realizations from simulated draws from copulas. These scatter diagrams are quite useful in illustrating tail dependence in a bivariate context. The capacity of copulas to generate extreme pairs of observations can be further emphasized by drawing a pair of lines parallel to the axes

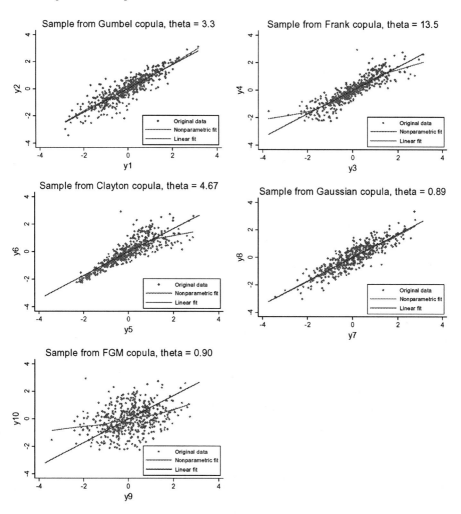

Fig. 2.2 Simulated samples from five copulas.

and noting the relative frequency of observations to the right or left of their intersection. Armstrong (2003) provides an interesting copula catalogue containing scatter plots for uniform pairs (u, v) drawn from specified copulas, and transformed normal pairs $(\Phi^{-1}(u), \Phi^{-1}(v))$.

Can scatter plots help in choosing a copula that is appropriate for modeling given data? When modeling is in terms of conditional marginals, that is, marginals that are conditioned on some covariates, the raw scatter diagrams have limited usefulness, as we shall see in Section 4.5. For example, the scatter diagrams for pairs of variables used in empirical applications (see, for example, Figure 2.2, top left panel) give us no clues as to which copula would work well. A better approach would be to first fit the marginals and derive marginal probabilities corresponding to (u, v), by employing the probability transform. Two-way scatter plots of these might be potentially useful in suggesting suitable copulas; see Figure 4.3.

To demonstrate dependence properties of different copulas, we follow an approach similar to that of Armstrong (2003). Nelsen (2006) also uses a similar graphical device. We simulate 500 pairs of uniform random variates from the Gumbel, Frank, Clayton, Gaussian, and FGM copulas using the approaches outlined in the Appendix. The uniform variables are converted to standard normal variables via the standard normal quantile function, $y_i = \Phi^{-1}(u_i)$ for $i = 1, 2$. The pairs of standard normal variates are plotted in order to illustrate dependence properties of the copulas. For four of the five copulas, the dependence parameter θ is set such that $\rho_\tau(y_1, y_2)$ equals 0.7. For the remaining copula, FGM, θ is set such that $\rho_\tau(y_1, y_2)$ equals 0.2, because FGM is unable to accommodate large dependence. Figure 2.3 displays five two-way scatters generated from simulated draws from the respective copulas.

Simulated variables from the Gaussian copula assume the familiar elliptical shape associated with the bivariate normal distribution. Dependence is symmetric in both tails of the distribution. Similarly, variables drawn from the Frank copula also exhibit symmetric dependence in both tails. However, compared to the Gaussian copula, dependence in the Frank copula is weaker in both tails, as is evident from the "fanning out" in the tails, and stronger in the center of the distribution. This suggests that the Frank copula is best suited for applications in which tail dependence is relatively weak.

In contrast to the Gaussian and Frank copulas, the Clayton and Gumbel copulas exhibit asymmetric dependence. Clayton dependence is strong in the left tail but weak in the right tail. The implication is that the Clayton copula is best suited for applications in which two outcomes are likely to experience low values together. On the other

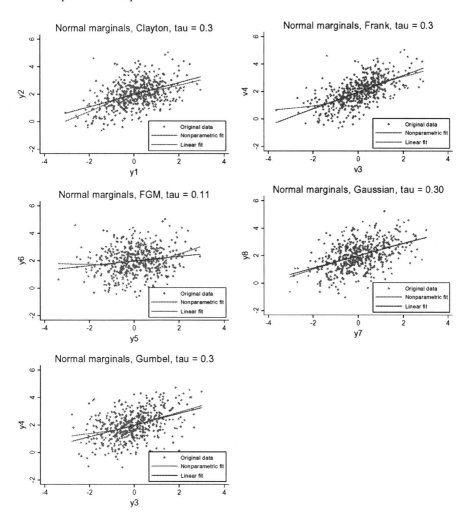

Fig. 2.3 Simulated samples from five conditional copulas.

hand, the Gumbel copula exhibits strong right tail dependence and weak left tail dependence, although the contrast between the two tails of the Gumbel copula is not as pronounced as in the Clayton copula. Consequently, as is well-known, Gumbel is an appropriate modeling choice when two outcomes are likely to simultaneously realize upper tail values.[1]

Finally, the FGM copula exhibits symmetry in both tails, but it cannot accommodate variables with large dependence. The FGM copula is popular in applied settings due to its simplicity and because it allows negative dependence, but it is only appropriate for applications with weak dependence. The implication of these graphs is that multivariate distributions with similar degrees of dependence might exhibit substantially different dependence structures. Understanding dependence structures of different copulas is imperative in empirical applications.

---

[1] For Gumbel, the degree of upper tail dependence is given by $2 - 2^{\theta}$. When Kendall's tau is 0.7, the Gumbel dependence parameter is $\theta = 3.33$. Thus, upper tail dependence is -8.06.

3

Generating Copulas

Copulas are useful for generating joint distributions with a variety of dependence structures. Because the selected copula restricts the dependence structure, no single copula will serve the practitioner well in all data situations. Hence it is desirable to have familiarity with a menu of available choices and their properties. So far in this article, we have covered a number of copulas that can be used to combine marginals. However, it is also desirable to avoid treating copulas in a blackbox fashion and to understand how copulas are related to other methods of generating joint distributions based on specified marginals. This requires an understanding of how copulas are generated. It is also useful to know how new families of copulas may be generated. In this section, we address this issue by considering some common approaches for generating copulas; for a deeper analysis based on characterizations of joint distributions see de la Peña et al. (2003).

A number of copulas were originally developed in specific contexts. A widely known example generates copulas through mixtures and compound distributions, e.g., Marshall and Olkin (1967, 1988), Hougaard (1987). Such mixtures arise naturally in specific contexts such as life times of spouses, twins, pairs of organs and so forth. Often these approaches generate dependence between variables through the presence of common unobserved heterogeneity. This seems attractive in most applications because it is impossible for observed covariates to cover all relevant aspects of an economic event. Because some copulas were developed for specific applications, they often embody restrictions that may have been appropriate in their original context but not when applied to other situations. It is often helpful, therefore, to know how the copulas are derived, at least for some widely used families.

Section 3.1 begins with the simplest of these, the **method of inversion,** which is based directly on Sklar's theorem. This method generates the copula from a given joint distribution. The examples illustrating inversion are not useful if our concern is to begin with marginals and derive a joint distribution by "copulation." This topic is discussed in Section 3.3. Section 3.4 introduces Archimedean copulas, and Section 3.5 considers issues of extending copulas to dimensions higher than two.

3.1   Method of Inversion

By Sklar's theorem, given continuous margins F_1 and F_2 and the joint continuous distribution function $F(y_1, y_2) = C(F_1(y_1), F_2(y_2))$, the corresponding copula is generated using the unique inverse transformations $y_1 = F_1^{-1}(u_1)$, and $y_2 = F_2^{-1}(u_2)$,

$$C(u_1, u_2) = F(F_1^{-1}(u_1), F_2^{-1}(u_2)),$$

where u_1 and u_2 are standard uniform variates. The same approach can be applied to the survival copula. Using, as before, the notation $\overline{F}$ for the joint survival function, and $\overline{F}_1$ and $\overline{F}_2$ for the marginal survival functions, the survival copula is given by $\overline{C}(u_1, u_2) = \overline{F}(\overline{F}_1^{-1}(u_1), \overline{F}_2^{-1}(u_2))$.

3.1.1   Examples of copulas generated by inversion

With a copula-based construction of a joint cdf, a set of marginals are combined to generate a joint cdf. Conversely, given a specification of a joint distribution, we can derive the corresponding unique copula. Consider the following bivariate example from Joe (1997: 13).

Beginning with the joint distribution, the two marginal distributions are derived as

$$F(y_1, y_2) = \exp\{-[e^{-y_1} + e^{-y_2} - (e^{-\theta y_1} + e^{-\theta y_2})^{-1/\theta}]\},$$
$$-\infty < y_1, y_2 < \infty, \quad \theta \geq 0 \tag{3.1}$$

$$\lim_{y_2 \to \infty} F(y_1, y_2) = F_1(y_1) = \exp(e^{-y_1}) \equiv u_1;$$

$$\lim_{y_1 \to \infty} F(y_1, y_2) = F_2(y_2) = \exp(e^{-y_2}) \equiv u_2;$$

hence $y_1 = -\log(-\log(u_1))$ and $y_2 = -\log(-\log(u_2))$. After substituting these expressions for y_1 and y_2 into the distribution function, the copula is

$$C(u_1, u_2) = u_1 u_2 \exp\{[(-\log u_1)^{-\theta} + (-\log u_2)^{-\theta}]^{-1/\theta}\}.$$

This expression can be rewritten as

$$C(u_1, u_2) = u_1 u_2 \phi^{-1}\{[(-\phi(u_1))^{-\theta} + (-\phi(u_2)^{-\theta})]^{-1/\theta}\}, \tag{3.2}$$

which will be seen to be a member of the **Archimedean class**. Beginning with the three joint distributions given in column 2 of the Table 3.1 given below and following a similar procedure, we can derive the three copulas in the last column. All three satisfy Properties 1 and 2 above. For Cases 1 and 2, setting $\theta = 0$ yields $F(y_1, y_2) = F(y_1) F(y_2)$ and $C(u_1, u_2) = u_1 u_2$, which is the case independence. That is, θ is a parameter that measures dependence. In Joe's example given above $\theta = 0$ implies independence and $\theta > 0$ implies dependence. In Case 3 the special case of independence is not possible.

Table 3.1 Selected joint distributions and their copulas.

Case	Joint distribution: $F(y_1, y_2)$	Margins: $F(y_1), F(y_2)$	Copula: $C(u_1, u_2)$
1	$1 - (e^{-\theta y_1} + e^{-2\theta y_2} - e^{-\theta(y_1 + 2y_2)})^{1/\theta}$	$F(y_1) = 1 - e^{-y_1}$	$1 - \{(1 - (1 - u_2)^\theta)(1 - u_1)^\theta$
	$\theta \geq 0$	$F(y_2) = 1 - e^{-2y_2}$	$+ (1 - u_2)^\theta\}^{1/\theta}$
2.	$\exp\{-(e^{-\theta y_1} + e^{-\theta y_2})^{1/\theta}\}$	$F(y_1) = \exp(-e^{-y_1})$;	$\exp\{-(-\ln u_1)^\theta$
			$+ (-\ln u_2)^\theta\}^{1/\theta}$
	$-\infty < y_1, y_2 < \infty, \theta \geq 1$	$F(y_2) = \exp(-e^{-y_2})$	
3.	$(1 + e^{-y_1} + e^{-y_2})^{-1}$	$F(y_1) = (1 + e^{-y_1})^{-1};$	$u_1 u_2 / (u_2 + u_1 - u_1 u_2)$
		$F(y_2) = (1 + e^{-y_2})^{-1}$	

An unattractive feature of the inversion method is that the joint distribution is required to derive the copula. This limits the usefulness of the inversion method for applications in which the researcher does not know the joint distribution.

3.2   Algebraic Methods

Some derivations of copulas begin with a relationship between marginals based on independence. Then this relationship is modified by introducing a dependence parameter and the corresponding copula is obtained. Nelsen calls this method "algebraic." Two examples of bivariate distributions derived by applying this method are the Plackett and Ali–Mikhail–Haq distributions. Here we show the derivation for the latter copula.

Example 3 in Table 3.1 is Gumbel's bivariate logistic distribution, denoted $F(y_1, y_2)$. Let $(1 - F(y_1, y_2))/F(y_1, y_2)$ denote the bivariate survival odds ratio by analogy with the univariate survival function. Then,

$$\frac{1 - F(y_1, y_2)}{F(y_1, y_2)} = e^{-y_1} + e^{-y_2}$$

$$= \frac{1 - F_1(y_1)}{F_1(y_1)} + \frac{1 - F_2(y_2)}{F_2(y_2)},$$

where $F_1(y_1)$ and $F_2(y_2)$ are univariate marginals. Observe that in this case there is no explicit dependence parameter.

In the case of independence, since $F(y_1, y_2) = F_1(y_1)F_2(y_2)$,

$$\frac{1 - F(y_1, y_2)}{F(y_1, y_2)} = \frac{1 - F_1(y_1)F_2(y_2)}{F_1(y_1)F_2(y_2)}$$

$$= \frac{1 - F_1(y_1)}{F_1(y_1)} + \frac{1 - F_2(y_2)}{F_2(y_2)} + \frac{1 - F_1(y_1)}{F_1(y_1)} \frac{1 - F_2(y_2)}{F_2(y_2)}.$$

Noting the similarity between the bivariate odds ratio in the dependence and independence cases, Ali, Mikhail, and Haq proposed a modified or generalized bivariate ratio with a dependence parameter θ:

$$\frac{1 - F(y_1, y_2)}{F(y_1, y_2)} = \frac{1 - F_1(y_1)}{F_1(y_1)} + \frac{1 - F_2(y_2)}{F_2(y_2)}$$
$$+ (1 - \theta)\frac{1 - F_1(y_1)}{F_1(y_1)}\frac{1 - F_2(y_2)}{F_2(y_2)}.$$

Then, defining $u_1 = F_1(y_1)$, $u_2 = F_2(y_2)$, and following the steps given in the preceding section, we obtain

$$\frac{1 - C(u_1, u_2; \theta)}{C(u_1, u_2; \theta)} = \frac{1 - u_1}{u_1} + \frac{1 - u_2}{u_2} + (1 - \theta)\frac{1 - u_1}{u_1}\frac{1 - u_2}{u_2},$$

whence

$$C(u_1, u_2; \theta) = \frac{u_1 u_2}{1 - \theta(1 - u_1)(1 - u_2)},$$

which, by introducing an explicit dependence parameter θ, extends the third example in Table 3.1.

3.3 Mixtures and Convex Sums

Given a copula C, its lower and upper bounds C_L and C_U, and the product copula $C^\perp$, a new copula can be constructed using a convex sum. Since, as was seen earlier, the upper Fréchet bound is always a copula, then for constant π_1, $0 \le \pi_1 \le 1$, the convex sum of the upper bound and independence copulas, denoted C^M,

$$C^M = \pi_1 C^\perp + (1 - \pi_1)C_U \tag{3.3}$$

is also a copula. This mixture copula is a special case of the class of Fréchet copulas, denoted C^F, defined as

$$C^F = \pi_1 C_L + (1 - \pi_1 - \pi_2)C^\perp + \pi_2 C_U, \tag{3.4}$$

where $0 \le \pi_1, \pi_2 \le 1$, and $\pi_1 + \pi_2 \le 1$.

A closely related idea considers copulas derived by averaging over an infinite collection of copulas indexed by a continuous variable η with a distribution function $\Lambda_\theta(\eta)$ with parameter θ. Specifically, the copula is obtained from the integral

$$C_\theta(u_1, u_2) = E_\eta[C_\eta(u_1, u_2)] = \int_{R(\eta)} C_\eta(u_1, u_2)d\Lambda_\theta(\eta).$$

This algebraic operation is usually referred to as mixing (with respect to η), leading to the mixture $C_\theta(u_1, u_2)$, which is also referred to as a **convex sum** (Nelsen, 2006).

Similarly, Marshall and Olkin (1988) consider the mixture

$$H(y) = \int [F(y)]^\eta d\Lambda(\eta), \quad \eta > 0. \tag{3.5}$$

They show that for any specified pair $\{H(y), \Lambda(\eta)\}, \overline{\Lambda}(0) = 1$, there exists $F(y)$ for which Eq. (3.5) holds. The right hand side can be written as $\varphi\,[-\ln F(y)]$, where φ is the Laplace transform of Λ, so $F(y) = \exp[-\varphi^{-1} H(y)]$.

A well known example from Marshall and Olkin (1988) illustrates how convex sums or mixtures lead to copulas constructed from Laplace transforms of distribution functions. Let $\varphi(t)$ denote the Laplace transform of a positive random (latent) variable η, also referred to as the mixing distribution Λ, i.e., $\varphi\,(t) = \int_0^\infty e^{-\eta t} d\Lambda(\eta)$. This is the moment generating function evaluated at $-t$. An inverse Laplace transform is an example of a generator. By definition, the Laplace transform of a positive random variable ν is

$$\mathcal{L}(t) = \mathrm{E}_\eta[e^{-t\eta}], \quad \eta > 0$$

$$= \int e^{-ts} dF_\eta(s) = \varphi(t),$$

hence $\varphi^{[-1]}\mathcal{L}(t) = t$. $\mathcal{L}(0) = 1$; $\mathcal{L}(t)$ is decreasing in t and always exists for $t \geq 0$.

Let $F_1(y_1) = \exp[-\varphi^{-1}(H_1(y_1))]$ and $F_2(y_2) = \exp[-\varphi^{-1}(H_2(y_2))]$ be some bench mark distribution functions for y_1 and y_2. Let the conditional distributions given a random variable η, $\eta > 0$, be $F_1(y_1|\eta) = [F_1(y_1)]^\eta$ and $F_2(y_2|\eta) = [F_2(y_2)]^\eta$. Then the mixture distribution,

$$H(y_1, y_2; \theta) = \int_0^\infty [F_1(y_1)]^\eta [F_2(y_2)]^\eta d\Lambda_\theta(\eta), \tag{3.6}$$

$$= \int_0^\infty \exp[-\eta[\varphi^{-1}(H_1(y_1)) + \varphi^{-1}(H_2(y_2))] d\Lambda_\theta(\eta),$$

$$= \varphi[\varphi^{-1}(H_1(y_1)) + \varphi^{-1}(H_2(y_2)); \theta],$$

(where the last line follows from the definition of the Laplace transform) is shown by Marshall and Olkin to be the joint distribution of (y_1, y_2) and it is also a (Archimedean) copula. $H_1(y_1)$ and $H_2(y_2)$ are the marginal distributions of $H(y_1, y_2; \theta)$. Observe that the copula involves the parameter θ, which measures dependence.

This method is often referred to as the "Marshall–Olkin method," and Joe (1997) refers to this as the **mixture of powers** method. An interpretation of this method is that it introduces an unobserved heterogeneity term η in the marginals. This is also referred to as "frailty" in the biostatistics literature. In the bivariate example given above, the same term enters both marginals. The distribution function of η depends upon an unknown parameter θ, which controls the dependence between y_1 and y_2 in their joint distribution.

The approach can be used more generally to derive higher dimensional Archimedean copulas. There are at least two possible variants, one in which the unobserved heterogeneity is common to all marginals, and another in which this term differs between marginals but the terms are jointly dependent. That is, the scalar η is replaced by a vector whose components (say η_1 and η_2) have a joint distribution, with one or more parameters that characterize dependence.

3.3.1 Examples

We give three examples of copulas generated by mixtures.

Dependence between stock indexes. Hu (2004) studies the dependence of monthly returns between four stock indexes: S&P 500, FTSE, Nikkei, and Hang Seng. She uses monthly averages from January 1970 to September 2003. She models dependence on a pair-wise basis using a finite mixture of three copulas (Gaussian (C_G), Gumbel (C_{Gumbel}) and Gumbel-Survival (C_{GS})):

$$C_{\text{mix}}(u, v; \rho, \alpha, \theta) = \pi_1 C_{\text{Gauss}}(u, v; \rho) + \pi_2 C_{\text{Gumbel}}(u, v; \alpha)$$
$$+ (1 - \pi_1 - \pi_2) C_{\text{GS}}(u, v; \theta).$$

Such a mixture imparts additional flexibility and also allows one to capture left and/or right tail dependence. Hu uses a two-step semiparametric approach in which empirical CDFs are used to model the marginals and maximum likelihood is used to estimate the dependence parameters ρ, α, and θ. Note that pairwise modeling of dependence can be potentially misleading if dependence is more appropriately captured by a higher dimensional model.

Dependence in lifetime data.   Marshall and Olkin (1967) introduce the common shock model in which the occurrence of a shock or disaster induces dependencies between otherwise independent lifetimes. Many of the earliest empirical applications to use copulas were in the area of survival analysis. An early example was Clayton (1978) who, in his study of joint lifetimes of fathers and sons, derives the joint survival function with shared frailty described by the gamma distribution. Dependence of lifetimes on pairs of individuals (father–son, husband–wife, twins) is well established. Oakes (1982) presents similar results in a random effects setting, and thus joint survival models of this form are often referred to as Clayton–Oakes models. Clayton and Cuzick (1985) develop an EM algorithm for estimating these models. In related work, Hougaard (1986) models joint survival times of groups of rats inflicted with tumors. Recent frailty models focus on joint survival times of family members, with particular interest devoted to annuity valuation. Frees et al. (1996) study joint- and last-survivor annuity contracts using Frank's copula. In a recent application, Wang (2003) studies survival times of bone marrow and heart transplant patients.

Many of these studies are based on the following specification. Consider the Cox proportional hazard regression model with the hazard rate $h(t|\mathbf{x}) = \exp(\mathbf{x}'\beta)h_0(t)$, where h_0 denotes the baseline hazard. Let η, $\eta > 0$, represent frailty (or unobserved heterogeneity) and denote the conditional survival function as $S(t \mid \eta)$. Then

$$S(t \mid \eta) = \exp[-H(t)]^\eta,$$

where $H(t)$ denotes the integrated baseline hazard. Let T_1 and T_2 denote lifetimes that are independent conditional on η. That is,

$$\begin{aligned}
\Pr[T_1 > t_1, T_2 > t_2|\eta] &= \Pr[T_1 > t_1|\eta]\Pr[T_2 > t_2|\eta] \\
&= S_1(t_1|\eta)S_2(t_2|\eta) \\
&= (\exp(-H_1(t_1)))^\eta(\exp(-H_2(t_2)))^\eta.
\end{aligned}$$

Integrating out η yields the bivariate distribution

$$\Pr[T_1 > t_1, T_2 > t_2] = E[(\exp(-H_1(t_1)))(\exp(-H_2(t_2)))]^\eta.$$

Different joint distributions are generated using different distributional assumptions about the conditionals and η. Hougaard et al. (1992) analyze joint survival of Danish twins born between 1881 and 1930 assuming Weibull conditionals and the assumption that η follows a positive stable distribution. Heckman and Honoré (1989) study the competing risks model.

Default and Claims Analysis. Financial analyses of credit risks are concerned with the possibility that a business may default on some financial obligation. If several firms or businesses are involved, each may be subject to a stochastic default arrival process. One way to model this is to consider time to default as a continuous random variable that can be analyzed using models for lifetime data, e.g., the Cox proportional hazard model. However, firms and businesses may face some common risks and shocks that create a potential for dependence in the distributions of time to default. Copulas can be used to model dependent defaults.

Li (2000) proposes the use of the Gaussian copula to analyze the joint distribution of m default times, denoted $T_1,\ldots,T_m$. The joint survival distribution can be expressed as a copula using Sklar's theorem:

$$S(t_1,\ldots,t_m) = \Pr[T_1 > t_1,\ldots,T_m > t_m]$$
$$= \overline{C}(S_1(t_1),\ldots,S_m(t_m)),$$

where $\overline{C}$ denotes the survival copula, see Section 2.2.

Suppose a random claims variable Y is exponentially distributed, conditional on a risk class ν,

$$\Pr[Y \leq y] = 1 - e^{-\nu y},$$

and let the risk class parameter ν be a gamma distributed variable with parameters (α,λ). Then the marginal distribution function for y is the Pareto distribution $F(y) = 1 - (1 + y/\lambda)^{-\alpha}$. For Y_1 and Y_2 in the same risk class, the joint distribution is

$$F(y_1,y_2) = 1 - \Pr[Y_1 > y_1] - \Pr[Y_2 > y_2] + \Pr[Y_1 > y_1, Y_2 > y_2]$$
$$= F_1(y_1) + F_2(y_2) - 1 + [(1 - F_1(y_1))^{-1/\alpha}$$
$$+ (1 - F_2(y_2))^{-1/\alpha} - 1]^{-\alpha}. \tag{3.7}$$

Observe that the right hand side is now a function of marginals and can be expressed as a copula. The right hand side can also be expressed in terms of marginal survival functions $S_1(y_1) = 1 - \Pr[Y_1 > y_1]$ and $S_2(y_{21}) = 1 - \Pr[Y_2 > y_2]$.

3.4 Archimedean copulas

A particular group of copulas that has proved useful in empirical modeling is the Archimedean class. Several members of this class have already been introduced above. Archimedean copulas are popular because they are easily derived and are capable of capturing wide ranges of dependence. This section discusses further aspects of Archimedean copulas and their properties, presents examples of popular Archimedean copulas, and illustrates their dependence characteristics.

3.4.1   Some properties of Archimedean copulas

Consider a class $\boldsymbol{\Phi}$ of functions $\varphi : [0,1] \rightarrow [0,\infty]$ with continuous derivatives on $(0,1)$ with the properties $\varphi(1) = 0$, $\varphi'(t) < 0$ (decreasing) and $\varphi''(t) > 0$ (convex) for all $0 < t < 1$, i.e., $\varphi(t)$ is a convex decreasing function. Further, let $\varphi(0) = \infty$ in the sense that $\lim_{t \to 0+} \varphi(t) = \infty$. These conditions ensure that an inverse φ^{-1} exists. Any function φ that satisfied these properties is capable of generating a bivariate distribution function; thus φ is referred to as a "generator function." For example, $\varphi(t) = -\ln(t)$, $\varphi(t) = (1 - t)^\theta$, and $\varphi(t) = t^{-\theta}$, $\theta > 1$, are members of the class. If $\varphi(0) = \infty$, the generator is said to be strict and its inverse exists. For strict generators $C(u_1, u_2) > 0$ except when $u_1 = 0$ or $u_2 = 0$. If $\varphi(0) < \infty$, the generator is not strict and its pseudo-inverse exists. In this case the copula has a singular component and takes the form $C(u_1, u_2) = \max[(.), 0]$. For example, consider $\varphi(t) = (1 - t)^\theta$, $\theta \in [1, \infty)$; this generates the copula $C(u_1, u_2) = \max[1 - [(1 - u_1)^\theta + (1 - u_2)^\theta]^{1/\theta}, 0]$. For a comparison of strict and non-strict generators, see Nelsen (2006: 113).

The inverse of the generator is written as φ^{-1} and its pseudo-inverse is written as $\varphi^{[-1]}$. The formal definition is

$$\varphi^{[-1]}(t) = \begin{cases} \varphi^{-1}(t) & 0 \leq t \leq \varphi(0) \\ 0 & \varphi(t) \leq t \leq +\infty \end{cases}$$

and

$$\varphi^{[-1]}(\varphi(t)) = t.$$

Bivariate Archimedean copulas without a singular component take the form:

$$C(u_1, u_2; \theta) = \varphi^{-1}(\varphi(u_1) + \varphi(u_2)), \qquad (3.8)$$

where the dependence parameter θ is imbedded in the functional form of the generator. Archimedean copulas are **symmetric** in the sense $C(u_1, u_2) = C(u_2, u_1)$ and **associative** in the sense $C(C(u_1, u_2), u_3) = C(u_1, C(u_2, u_3))$.

The density of the bivariate Archimedean copula is

$$c_{u_1 u_2} = \frac{\varphi''(C(u_1, u_2))\varphi'(u_1)\varphi'(u_2)}{[\varphi'(C(u_1, u_2))]^3}, \qquad (3.9)$$

where the derivatives do not exist on the boundary $\varphi(u_1) + \varphi(u_2) = \varphi(0)$; see Genest and Mackay (1986) for a derivation.

The conditional density of the Archimedean copula is

$$\frac{\partial}{\partial u_2} C(u_1, u_2) = \frac{\varphi'(u_2)}{\varphi'(C(u_1, u_2))}, \qquad (3.10)$$

which is obtained by differentiating (3.8) with respect to u_2 and rearranging the result.

Different generator functions yield different Archimedean copulas when plugged into Eq. (3.8). For example, consider the generator $\varphi(t) = -\ln(t), 0 \leq t \leq 1$; then $\varphi(0) = \infty$, $\varphi^{[-1]}(t) = \exp(-t)$. Then (3.8) reduces to $C(u_1, u_2) = uv$, the product copula. Consider the generator $\varphi(t; \theta) = \ln(1 - \theta \ln t), 0 \leq \theta \leq 1$; then $\varphi^{[-1]}(t) = \exp((1 - e^t)/\theta)$. Then (3.8) reduces to $C(u_1, u_2; \theta) = uv \exp(-\theta \ln(u_1) \ln(u_2))$. For econometric modeling it is not clear that nonstrict generators have any specific advantages. Some authors only use strict generators, e.g., see Smith (2005).

The properties of the generator affect tail dependency of the Archimedean copula. If $\varphi'(0) < \infty$ and $\varphi'(0) \neq 0$, then $C(u_1, u_2)$ does not have the RTD property. If $C(\cdot)$ has the RTD property then $1/\varphi'(0) = -\infty$. See Cherubini et al. (2004, Theorem 3.12). Marshall and Olkin (1988) results given in the preceding section show that Archimedean copulas are easily generated using inverse Laplace transformations. Since Laplace transformations have well-defined inverses, φ^{-1} serves as a generator function.

Quantifying dependence is relatively straightforward for Archimedean copulas because Kendall's tau simplifies to a function of the generator function,

$$\tau = 1 + 4 \int_0^1 \frac{\varphi(t)}{\varphi'(t)} dt, \tag{3.11}$$

see Genest and Mackay (1986) for a derivation.

3.4.2   Archimedean copulas extended by transformations

In some cases additional flexibility arising from a second parameter in the copula may be empirically useful. The method of transformations has been suggested as a way of attaining such flexibility; see Durrleman et al. (2000) and Junker and May (2005). Additional flexibility results from the presence of a free parameter in the transformation function. The essential step is to find valid new generators, and this can be accomplished using transformations.

Junker and May (2005) prove the following result. Let φ be a generator and $g : [0,1] \rightarrow [0,1]$ be a strictly increasing concave function with $g(1) = 1$. Then $\varphi \circ g$ is a generator. Let $f : [0,\infty] \rightarrow [0,\infty]$ be a strictly increasing convex function with $f(0) = 0$, then $f \circ \varphi$ is a generator. Here f and g are transformations applied to the original generator φ. Examples of transformations given by Junker and May, some of which have previously appeared in the literature, include:

$$g(t) = t^\nu, \qquad \nu \in (0,1)$$
$$g(t) = \frac{\ln(at + 1)}{\ln(a + 1)}, \qquad a \in (0,\infty)$$

$$g(t) = \frac{e^{-\theta t} - 1}{e^{-\theta} - 1}, \qquad \theta \in (-\infty,\infty)$$
$$f(\varphi) = \varphi^\delta, \qquad \delta \in (1,\infty)$$
$$f(\varphi) = a^\varphi - 1, \qquad a \in (1,\infty)$$
$$f(\varphi) = a^{-\varphi} - 1, \qquad a \in (0,1).$$

As an example, the Frank copula is derived from the generator $\varphi(t) = -\log\left[(e^{-\theta t} - 1)/(e^{-\theta} - 1)\right]$. This copula can be extended by using the transformed generator $[\varphi(t)]^{\delta}$, so the Frank copula is a special case when $\delta = 1$.

3.4.3 Examples of Archimedean copulas

The appeal of Archimedean copulas and the reason for their popularity in empirical applications is that Eq. (3.8) produces wide ranges of dependence properties for different choices of the generator function. Archimedean copulas are also relatively easy to estimate. There are dozens of existing Archimedean copulas (see Hutchinson and Lai (1990) for a fairly exhaustive list), and infinitely more that could be developed (if some assumptions are relaxed). Table 3.2 lists three that appear regularly in statistics literature: Frank, Clayton, and Gumbel. For Clayton, two cases are listed, corresponding to strict and non-strict generators, the latter with analytic continuation at the origin, which makes it comprehensive. These three copulas, as discussed in Section 2.3, are popular because they accommodate different patterns of dependence and have relatively straightforward functional forms. Table 3.3 shows several copula densities.

3.5 Extensions of Bivariate Copulas

With a few exceptions, copulas are usually applied to bivariate data, and only one dependence parameter is estimated. We briefly discuss methods for estimating systems with three or more dependent variables, and copulas with more than one dependence parameter.

Ideally, an m-variate copula would have $m(m - 1)/2$ dependence parameters, one for each bivariate marginal. The most obvious choice is the Gaussian copula discussed by Lee (1983), which can be extended to include additional marginal distributions. The covariance structure of the multivariate normal distribution has $m(m - 1)/2$ dependence parameters. However, implementing a multivariate normal copula requires calculation of multiple integrals without closed form solutions, which must be approximated numerically. Husler and Reiss (1989), Joe (1990), and Joe (1994) propose multivariate copulas with flexible

Table 3.2 Selected Archimedean copulas and their generators.

	$C(u_1, u_2; \theta)$	$\varphi(t)$	Range of θ
Clayton	$(u_1^{-\theta} + u_2^{-\theta} - 1)^{-1/\theta}$	$\theta^{-1}(t^{-\theta} - 1)$ (strict)	$(0, \infty)$
Clayton	$[\max(u_1^{-\theta} + u_2^{-\theta} - 1, 0)]^{-1/\theta}$	$\theta^{-1}(t^{-\theta} - 1)$ (nonstrict)	$(-1, \infty) \backslash \{0\}$
Frank	$-\frac{1}{\theta} \log \left(1 + \frac{(e^{-\theta u_1} - 1)(e^{-\theta u_2} - 1)}{e^{-\theta} - 1} \right)$	$-\log \left[(e^{-\theta t} - 1)/(e^{-\theta} - 1) \right]$	$(-\infty, \infty)$
Gumbel	$\exp \left(-(\tilde{u}_1^\theta + \tilde{u}_2^\theta)^{1/\theta} \right)$ where $\tilde{u}_j = -\log u_j$	$(-\log t)^\theta$	$[1, \infty)$

Table 3.3 Selected copula densities.

Copula	$C(u_1, u_2)$	$C_{12}(u_1, u_2)$
FGM	$u_1 u_2 \left(1 + \theta(1 - u_1)(1 - u_2)\right)$	$1 + \theta(1 - 2u_1)(1 - 2u_2)$
Gaussian	$\Phi_G\left(\Phi^{-1}(u_1), \Phi^{-1}(u_2); \theta\right)$	$(1 - \theta^2)^{-1/2} \exp\left\{-\frac{1}{2}(1 - \theta^2)^{-1}\left(x^2 + y^2 - 2\theta xy\right)\right\}$ $\times \exp\left\{\frac{1}{2}\left(x^2 + y^2\right)\right\}$ where $x = \Phi^{-1}(u_1)$, $y = \Phi^{-1}(u_2)$
Clayton	$\left(u_1^{-\theta} + u_2^{-\theta} - 1\right)^{-1/\theta}$	$(1 + \theta)(u_1 u_2)^{-\theta-1}\left(u_1^{-\theta} + u_2^{-\theta} - 1\right)^{-2-1/\theta}$
Frank	$-\frac{1}{\theta}\log\left(1 + \frac{(e^{-\theta u_1} - 1)(e^{-\theta u_2} - 1)}{e^{-\theta} - 1}\right)$	$\dfrac{-\theta(e^{-\theta} - 1)e^{-\theta(u_1+u_2)}}{\left((e^{-\theta u_1} - 1)(e^{-\theta u_2} - 1) + (e^{\theta} - 1)\right)^2}$
Gumbel	$\exp\left\{-\left(\widetilde{u_1}^\theta + \widetilde{u_2}^\theta\right)^{1/\theta}\right\}$	$C(u_1, u_2)(u_1 u_2)^{-1}\dfrac{(\widetilde{u_1}\widetilde{u_2})^{\theta-1}}{(\widetilde{u_1}^\theta + \widetilde{u_2}^\theta)^{2-1/\theta}}\left[\left(\widetilde{u_1}^\theta + \widetilde{u_2}^\theta\right)^{1/\theta} + \theta - 1\right]$, where $\widetilde{u_1} = -\ln u_1$, and $\widetilde{u_2} = -\ln u_2$

dependence, but their models either require Monte Carlo numerical integration or they perform poorly in empirical applications.

3.5.1   Multivariate extensions using Marshall–Olkin's results

Consider an extension of the Marshall–Olkin method to dimensions > 2. The following statement follows Marshall and Olkin (1988) Theorem 2.1.

Let $H_1, \ldots, H_m$ be univariate distribution functions, and let Λ be an m-variate distribution function such that $\Lambda(0, \ldots, 0) = 1$ with univariate marginals $\Lambda_1, \ldots, \Lambda_m$. Denote the Laplace transform of Λ and Λ_i, respectively, by φ and φ_i $(i = 1, \ldots, m)$. Let K be an m-variate distribution function with all marginals uniform on $[0, 1]$.

If $F_i(y) = \exp[-\varphi_i^{-1} H_i(y)]$, then

$$H(y_1, \ldots, y_m) = \int \cdots \int K([F_1(y_1)]^{\eta_1}, \ldots, [F_m(y_m)]^{\eta_m}) d\Lambda(\eta_1, \ldots, \eta_m)$$

is an m-dimensional distribution function with marginals $H_1, \ldots, H_m$.

A special case of this theorem occurs when $K([F_1(y_1)]^{\eta_1}, \ldots, [F_m(y_m)]^{\eta_m}) = \Pi_{i=1}^m F_i(y_i)]^{\eta_i}$ and the y_i $(i = 1, \ldots, m)$ are uniform $[0, 1]$ variates. In this case the application of the theorem yields the m-dimensional copula

$$H(y_1, \ldots, y_m) = \varphi[\varphi_1^{-1} H_1(y_1), \ldots, \varphi_m^{-1} H_m(y_m)].$$

A further specialization occurs if we assume, in addition, that all univariate marginals $\Lambda_1, \ldots, \Lambda_m$ are identical and have an upper Fréchet–Hoeffding bound Λ_1, with Laplace transform φ. In this case the joint distribution function is

$$H(y_1, \ldots, y_m) = \varphi[\varphi_1^{-1} H_1(y_1) + \cdots + \varphi_m^{-1} H_m(y_m)],$$

which extends the Archimedean form to m-dimensions. This result also extends to the case in which the marginals are univariate survival functions. Thus, the extension to higher dimensions requires the assumption that all conditional distributions depend on a common random variable which enters the conditional as a power term. Then a single parameter will characterize dependence between all pairs of variables. This is clearly restrictive in the context of fitting copulas to data.

Different choices of H_i and Λ lead to different generators φ and to different copulas. Marshall and Olkin (1988) give examples covering five alternative sets of assumptions. Genest and Mackay (1986) explain that, for the case of $m = 2$, φ can be a function different from a Laplace transform. However, for extension to higher dimensions, due to a result of Schweizer and Sklar (1983) (see Marshall and Olkin, 1988: 835), the generator must be proportional to a Laplace transform. Thus, from the viewpoint of one who wants to fit copulas to data, the use of the mixtures method for the $m > 2$ case involves significant restrictions.

3.5.2   Method of nesting

Archimedean copulas can be extended to include additional marginal distributions. Focusing on the trivariate case, the easiest method by which to include a third marginal is

$$C(u_1, u_2, u_3) = \varphi\left(\varphi^{-1}(u_1) + \varphi^{-1}(u_2) + \varphi^{-1}(u_3)\right). \tag{3.12}$$

This construction can be readily used in empirical applications, but it is restrictive because it is necessary to assume that φ^{-1} is completely monotonic (Cherubini et al., 2004: 149), and because the specification implies symmetric dependence between the three pairs $(u_1, u_2), (u_2, u_3)$, and (u_1, u_3), due to having a single dependence parameter. This restriction becomes more onerous as the number of marginals increases. It is not possible to model separately the dependence between all pairs.

The functional form of an Archimedean copula will be recognized by those familiar with the theory of separable and additively separable functions. A function $f(u_1, u_2, \ldots, u_m)$ is (weakly) separable if it can be written as

$$f(u_1, u_2, \ldots, u_m) = \phi\{\phi^1(\mathbf{u}_1), \ldots, \phi^Q(\mathbf{u}_Q)\},$$

and additively separable if

$$f(u_1, u_2, \ldots, u_m) = \phi\left\{\sum_{q=1}^{Q} \phi^q(\mathbf{u}_q)\right\},$$

where $(\mathbf{u}_1, \ldots, \mathbf{u}_Q)$ is a separation of the set of variables $(u_1, u_2, \ldots, u_m)$ into Q nonoverlapping groups. A function may be separable but not additively separable. Many Archimedean copulas are additively separable. Under separability variables can be nested. For example if $m = 3$, then the following groupings are possible: $(u_1, u_2, u_3; \theta)$; $(u_1, [u_2, u_3; \theta_2]; \theta_1)$; $(u_2, [u_1, u_3; \theta_2]; \theta_1)$; $(u_3, [u_1, u_2; \theta_2]; \theta_1)$. When fitting copulas to data, the alternative groupings have different implications and interpretations. Presumably each grouping is justified by some set of assumptions about dependence. The first grouping restricts the dependence parameter θ to be the same for all pairs. The remaining three groupings allow for two dependence parameters, one, θ_1, for a pair and a second one, θ_2, for dependence between the singleton and the pair. The existence of generators ϕ^q that lead to flexible forms of Archimedean copulas seems to be an open question. Certain types of extensions to multivariate copulas are not possible. For example, Genest et al. (1995) considered a copula C such that

$$H(x_1, x_2, \ldots, x_m, y_1, y_2, \ldots, y_n) = C(F(x_1, x_2, \ldots, x_m), G(y_1, y_2, \ldots, y_n))$$

defines a $(m + n)$-dimensional distribution function with marginals F and G, $m + n \geq 3$. They found that the only copula consistent with these marginals is the independence copula. Multivariate Archimedean copulas with a single dependence parameter can be obtained if restrictions are placed on the generator. For multivariate generalizations of Gumbel, Frank and Clayton, see Cherubini et al. (2004: 150–151). Copula densities for dimensions higher than 2 are tedious to derive; however, Cherubini et al. (2004, Section 7.5) gives a general expression for the Clayton copula density, and for the Frank copula density for the special case of four variables.

We exploit the mixtures of powers method to extend Archimedean copulas to include a third marginal. For a more detailed exposition of this method, see Joe (1997, ch. 5) and Zimmer and Trivedi (2006). The trivariate mixtures of powers representation is

$$C(u_1, u_2, u_3) = \int_0^\infty \int_0^\infty G^\beta(u_1) G^\beta(u_2) dM_2(\beta; \alpha) G^\alpha(u_3) dM_1(\alpha),$$

(3.13)

where $G(u_1) = \exp(-\phi^{-1}(u_1))$, $G(u_2) = \exp(-\phi^{-1}(u_2))$, $G(u_3) = \exp(-\varphi^{-1}(u_3))$, and φ is a Laplace transformation. In this formulation, the power term α affects u_1, u_2, and u_3, and a second power term β

affects u_1 and u_2. The distribution M_1 has Laplace transformation $\varphi(\cdot)$, and M_2 has Laplace transformation $\left((\varphi^{-1} \circ \phi)^{-1}(-\alpha^{-1}\log(\cdot))\right)^{-1}$. When $\phi = \varphi$, expression (3.13) simplifies to expression (3.12). (The mathematical notation $f \circ g$ denotes the functional operation $f(g(x))$.) When $\phi \neq \varphi$, the trivariate extension of (3.8) corresponding to (3.13) is

$$C(u_1, u_2, u_3) = \varphi\left(\varphi^{-1} \circ \phi[\phi^{-1}(u_1) + \phi^{-1}(u_2)] + \varphi^{-1}(u_3)\right). \quad (3.14)$$

Therefore, different Laplace transformations produce different families of trivariate copulas.

Expression (3.12) has symmetric dependence in the sense that it produces one dependence parameter $\theta = \theta_{u_1 u_2} = \theta_{u_1 u_3} = \theta_{u_2 u_3}$. But the dependence properties of three different marginals are rarely symmetric in empirical applications. The trivariate representation of expression (3.14) is symmetric with respect to (u_1, u_2) but not with respect to u_3. Therefore, (3.14) is less restrictive than (3.12).

The partially symmetric formulation of expression (3.14) yields two dependence parameters, θ_1 and θ_2, such that $\theta_1 \leq \theta_2$. The parameter $\theta_2 = \theta_{u_1 u_2}$ measures dependence between u_1 and u_2. The parameter $\theta_1 = \theta_{u_1 u_3} = \theta_{u_2 u_3}$ measures dependence between u_1 and u_3 as well as between u_2 and u_3, and the two must be equal. Distributions greater than three dimensions also have a mixtures of powers representations, but this technique yields only $m - 1$ dependence parameters for an m-variate distribution function. Therefore, the mixtures of powers approach is more restrictive for higher dimensions. While this restriction constitutes a potential weakness of the approach, it is less restrictive than formulation (3.12) which yields only one dependence parameter. Moreover, the multivariate representation in Eq. (3.14) allows a researcher to explore several dependence patterns by changing the ordering of the marginals. For example, instead of (u_1, u_2, u_3), one could order the marginals (u_3, u_2, u_1), which provides a different interpretation for the two dependence parameters.

As an example, we demonstrate how the Frank copula is extended to include a third marginal. If $\phi(s) = \exp(-s^{1/\theta})$ and $(\varphi^{-1} \circ \phi)(s)$

$= s^{\theta_1/\theta_2}$, then expression (3.14) becomes

$$C(u_1, u_2, u_3; \theta_1, \theta_2)$$

$$= -\theta_1 \log \left\{ 1 - c_1^{-1} \left(\begin{array}{c} 1 - [1 - c_2^{-1}(1 - e^{-\theta_2 u_1}) \\ \times (1 - e^{-\theta_2 u_2})]^{\theta_1/\theta_2} \end{array} \right) (1 - e^{-\theta_1 u_3}) \right\},$$

$$(3.15)$$

where $\theta_1 \leq \theta_2$, $c_1 = 1 - e^{-\theta_1}$, and $c_2 = 1 - e^{-\theta_2}$. (The proof is complicated; see Joe (1993).) Despite the ability of some bivariate Archimedean copulas to accommodate negative dependence, trivariate Archimedean copulas derived from mixtures of powers restrict θ_1 and θ_2 to be greater than zero, which implies positive dependence. This reflects an important property of mixtures of powers. In order for the integrals in Eq. (3.13) to have closed form solutions, then power terms α and β, which are imbedded within θ_1 and θ_2, must be positive.

Trivariate example.   Zimmer and Trivedi (2006) develop a trivariate model in which y_1 and y_2 are counted measures of health care use by two spouses and y_3 is a dichotomous variable of insurance status. One group consists of couples who are insured jointly, and a second group consists of married couples where wife and husband are separately insured. The interest is in determining the impact of y_3 on y_1 and y_2. They exploit the mixtures of powers representation to extend the (Frank) copula to include a third marginal. Specifically they use (3.14) which is somewhat less restrictive than the trivariate Archimedean copula $\phi\left(\phi^{-1}(u_1) + \phi^{-1}(u_2) + \phi^{-1}(u_3)\right)$. The latter has symmetric dependence in the sense that it produces one dependence parameter for all pairs of marginals. The nested Archimedean form has symmetric with respect to (u_1, u_2), but not with respect to u_3.

3.5.3   Copulas with two dependence parameters

Although they are rarely used in empirical applications, it is possible to construct Archimedean copulas with two dependence parameters, each of which measures a different dependence feature. For example, one parameter might measure left tail dependence while the other might measure right tail dependence. The bivariate Student's t-distribution was mentioned earlier as an example of a two-parameter copula. Transformation copulas in Section 3.4 are a second example. Two parameter Archimedean copulas take the form:

$$C(u_1, u_2) = \varphi\left(-\log K\left(e^{-\varphi(u_1)}, e^{-\varphi(u_2)}\right)\right), \qquad (3.16)$$

where K is max-id and φ is a Laplace transformation. If K assumes an Archimedean form, and if K has dependence parameter θ_1, and φ is parameterized by θ_2, then $C(u_1, u_2; \theta_1, \theta_2)$ assumes an Archimedean form with two dependence parameters. Joe (1997: 149–154) discusses this calculation in more detail. As an example, we present one Archimedean copula with two parameters, and we direct the interested reader to Joe (1997) for more examples.

If K assumes the Gumbel form, then (3.16) takes the form:

$$C(u_1, u_2; \theta_1, \theta_2) = \varphi\left(\varphi^{-1}(u_1) + \varphi^{-1}(u_2)\right),$$

where $\varphi(t) = (1 + t^{1/\theta_1})^{-1/\theta_2}$, $\theta_2 > 0$ and $\theta_1 \geq 1$. For this copula, $2^{-1/(\theta_1\theta_2)}$ measures lower tail dependence and $2 - 2^{1/\theta_1}$ captures upper tail dependence.

4

Copula Estimation

Copulas are used to model dependence when the marginal distributions are conditional on covariates, i.e., they have a regression structure, and also when they are not. Sometimes the investigator's main interest is in efficient estimation of regression parameters and only incidentally in the dependence parameter. In models which do not involve covariates, the main interest is, of course, in the nature of dependence.

Simultaneous estimation of all parameters using the full maximum likelihood (**FML**) approach is the most direct estimation method. A second method is a sequential 2-step maximum likelihood method (**TSML**) in which the marginals are estimated in the first step and the dependence parameter is estimated in the second step using the copula after the estimated marginal distributions have been substituted into it. This method exploits an attractive feature of copulas for which the dependence structure is independent of the marginal distributions. This second method has additional variants depending upon whether the first step is implemented parametrically or nonparametrically, and on the method used to estimate the variance of the dependence parameter(s) at the second stage. A third method that is in principle feasible, but not yet widely used in practice, is to estimate the parameters using the generalized method of moments (**GMM**); this, however, requires one to first derive the moment functions. (See Prokhorov and Schmidt, 2006, for a discussion of theoretical issues related to copula estimation.) In the remainder of this section we will concentrate on the FML and TSML methods.

In what follows we will treat the case of copulas of continuous variables as the leading case. For generality we consider copulas in which each marginal distribution, denoted as $F_j(y_j|\mathbf{x}_j; \beta_j), j = 1, \ldots, m$, is conditioned on a vector covariates denoted as $\mathbf{x}_j$. In most cases, unless specified otherwise $m = 2$, and F_j is parametrically specified. In most cases we will assume that the dependence parameter, denoted θ, is a scalar.

Sections 4.1 and 4.2 cover the full maximum likelihood and the two-step sequential maximum likelihood methods. Section 4.3 covers model evaluation and selection. Monte Carlo examples and real data examples are given in Sections 4.4 and 4.5.

4.1   Copula Likelihoods

Having chosen a copula consider the derivation of the likelihood for the special case of a bivariate model with uncensored failure times (y_1, y_2). Denote the marginal density functions as $f_j(y_j|\mathbf{x}_j; \beta_j) = \partial F_j$ $(y_j|\mathbf{x}_j; \beta_j)/\partial y_j$ and the copula derivative as $C_j((F_1|\mathbf{x}_1; \beta_1), (F_2|\mathbf{x}_1; \beta_1); \theta)/\partial F_j$ for $j = 1, 2$. Then the copula density is

$$
\begin{aligned}
c(F_1(\cdot), F_2(\cdot)) &= \frac{d}{dy_2 dy_1} C(F_1(\cdot), F_2(\cdot)) \\
&= C_{12}(F_1(\cdot), F_2(\cdot)) f_1(\cdot) f_2(\cdot),
\end{aligned} \tag{4.1}
$$

where

$$
C_{12}((F_1|\mathbf{x}_1; \beta_1), (F_2|\mathbf{x}_2; \beta_2); \theta) = \partial C((F_1|\mathbf{x}_1; \beta_1), (F_2|\mathbf{x}_2; \beta_2); \theta)/\partial F_1 \partial F_2, \tag{4.2}
$$

and the log-likelihood function is

$$
\begin{aligned}
\mathcal{L}_N(y_1|&(\mathbf{x}_1; \beta_1), (y_2|\mathbf{x}_2; \beta_2); \theta) \\
&= \sum_{i=1}^{N} \sum_{j=1}^{2} \ln f_{ji}(y_{ji}|\mathbf{x}_{ji}; \beta_j) \\
&\quad + \sum_{i=1}^{N} C_{12}[F_1(y_{1i}|\mathbf{x}_{1i}; \beta_1), F_2(y_{2i}|\mathbf{x}_{2i}; \beta_2); \theta].
\end{aligned} \tag{4.3}
$$

The cross partial derivatives $C_{12}(\cdot)$ for several copulas are listed below. It is easy to see that the log-likelihood decomposes into two parts, of which only the second involves the dependence parameter.

$$\mathcal{L}_N(\beta_1, \beta_2, \theta) = \mathcal{L}_{1,N}(\beta_1, \beta_2) + \mathcal{L}_{2,N}(\beta_1, \beta_2, \theta). \tag{4.4}$$

FML estimates are obtained by solving the score equations $\partial \mathcal{L}_N / \partial \boldsymbol{\Omega} = \boldsymbol{0}$ where $\boldsymbol{\Omega} = (\beta_1, \beta_2, \theta)$. These equations will be nonlinear in general, but standard quasi-Newton iterative algorithms are available in most matrix programming languages. Let the solution be $\widehat{\boldsymbol{\Omega}}_{\mathrm{FML}}$. By standard likelihood theory under regularity conditions, $\widehat{\boldsymbol{\Omega}}_{\mathrm{FML}}$ is consistent for the true parameter vector $\boldsymbol{\Omega}_0$ and its asymptotic distribution is given by

$$\sqrt{N}(\widehat{\boldsymbol{\Omega}}_{\mathrm{FML}} - \boldsymbol{\Omega}_0) \xrightarrow{d} \mathcal{N}\left[\boldsymbol{0}, -\left(\mathrm{plim}\frac{1}{N}\frac{\partial^2 \mathcal{L}_N(\boldsymbol{\Omega})}{\partial \boldsymbol{\Omega} \partial \boldsymbol{\Omega}'}\bigg|\right)^{-1}_{\boldsymbol{\Omega}_0}\right]. \tag{4.5}$$

In practice the more robust consistent "sandwich" variance estimator, obtained under quasi-likelihood theory, may be preferred as it allows for possible misspecification of the copula.

4.1.1 Likelihood maximization by parts

There is an alternative computational strategy for obtaining $\widehat{\boldsymbol{\Omega}}_{\mathrm{FML}}$. In view of the structure of the log-likelihood, see (4.4), one can use the **maximization-by-parts (MBP)** algorithm recently suggested by Song et al. (2005). This involves starting from an initial estimate of (β_1, β_2) based on maximization of $\mathcal{L}_{1,N}(\beta_1, \beta_2)$, and then using Eq. (4.4) to solve for θ. The initial estimate ignores dependence, and hence is not efficient. An iterative solution for (β_1, β_2) given an estimate θ, and then for θ given revised estimates of (β_1, β_2), yields efficient estimates because the procedure takes account of dependence. If there is no dependence, then the first step estimator is efficient. Song et al. (2005) illustrate the MBP algorithm by estimating a bivariate Gaussian copula.

Likelihoods also may be expressed in alternative forms using **associated copulas**, e.g. survival copulas, as defined in Section 2.2. Such alternative expressions are often convenient when handling models with censored observations (see Frees and Valdez, 1998: 15–16, Georges et al., 2001).

4.1.2 Copula for discrete variables

To illustrate the case of discrete random variables, we consider the case in which y_1 and y_2 are nonnegative integer (count) variables and F_1 and F_2 are discrete cdfs. The joint probability mass function (pmf) is formed by taking differences. For economy, we use the abbreviated notation $F_j(y_j)$ for $F_j(y_j|\mathbf{x}_j, \beta_j)$. For the bivariate case, the probability mass function (pmf) is

$$
\begin{aligned}
c(F_1(y_{1i}), F_2(y_{2i}); \theta) = {} & C(F_1(y_{1i}), F_2(y_{2i}); \theta) \\
& - C(F_1(y_{1i} - 1), F_2(y_{2i}); \theta) \\
& - C(F_1(y_{1i}), F_2(y_{2i} - 1); \theta) \\
& + C(F_1(y_{1i} - 1), F_2(y_{2i} - 1); \theta). \quad (4.6)
\end{aligned}
$$

For the trivariate case the pmf is

$$
\begin{aligned}
c(F_1(y_{1i}), & F_2(y_{2i}), F_3(y_{3i}); \theta) \\
= {} & C(F_1(y_{1i}), F_2(y_{2i}), F_3(y_{3i}); \theta) \\
& - C(F_1(y_{1i} - 1), F_2(y_{2i}), F_3(y_{3i}); \theta) \\
& - C(F_1(y_{1i}), F_2(y_{2i} - 1), F_3(y_{3i}); \theta) \\
& - C(F_1(y_{1i}), F_2(y_{2i}), F_3(y_{3i} - 1); \theta) \\
& + C(F_1(y_{1i} - 1), F_2(y_{2i} - 1), F_3(y_{3i}); \theta) \\
& + C(F_1(y_{1i}), F_2(y_{2i} - 1), F_3(y_{3i} - 1); \theta) \\
& + C(F_1(y_{1i} - 1), F_2(y_{2i}), F_3(y_{3i} - 1); \theta) \\
& - C(F_1(y_{1i} - 1), F_2(y_{2i} - 1), F_3(y_{3i} - 1); \theta). \quad (4.7)
\end{aligned}
$$

Focusing on the bivariate case, the log likelihood function for FML estimation is formed by taking the logarithm of the pdf or pmf copula representation and summing over all observations,

$$
\mathcal{L}_N(\theta) = \sum_{i=1}^{N} \log c(F_1(y_{1i}), F_2(y_{2i}); \theta). \quad (4.8)
$$

As was discussed in Section 2.4, the interpretation of the dependence parameter θ in the context of discrete data is not identical to that in the corresponding continuous case. If there is special interest in estimating and interpreting the dependence parameter, an alternative to estimating the discrete copula is to apply the continuation transformation to the discrete variable and then base the estimation of parameters on the likelihood function for a family of continuous copulas. Specifically, the discrete variables are made continuous by adding a random independent perturbation term taking values in $[0, 1]$. This approach was used by Stevens (1950), and, as was mentioned above, by Denuit and Lambert (2005) to derive bounds for Kendall's ρ_τ measure, and by Machado and Santos Silva (2005) to extend quantile regression to count data.

In our experience, maximization of likelihood with discrete margins often runs into computational difficulties, reflected in the failure of the algorithm to converge. In such cases it may be helpful to first apply the continuation transformation and then estimate a model based on copulas for continuous variables. For example, count variables can be made continuous and then suitable margins inserted in a specified copula. Examples are given in Sections 4.4.2 and 4.5.2.

4.1.3 Bayesian analysis of copulas

There is now growing interest in Bayesian analysis of copulas. A recent example is Pitt et al. (2006), who use a Gaussian copula to model the joint distribution of six count measures of health care. The multivariate density of the Gaussian copula has been given by Song (2000). The text by Pitt et al. (2006) develops a Markov chain Monte Carlo algorithm for estimating the posterior distribution for continuous or discrete marginals. In their application the marginal densities are specified to be zero-inflated geometric distributions. The authors show how one might handle the additional complications resulting from discrete marginals.

4.2 Two-Step Sequential Likelihood Maximization

The TSML method separates the estimation of the marginals from that of the dependence parameter. We shall consider two cases. In the first the marginal distributions do not involve covariates and the density is not parametrically specified either because it is preferred to avoid doing so, or because this step is too difficult.

4.2.1   Nonparametric first step

Consider the case of continuous random variables. A nonparametric kernel density is used to estimate the univariate marginal densities, denoted $\widehat{f}_j(y_j)$, $j = 1, 2$. This usually requires one to choose a bandwidth parameter. This is used to compute the empirical distribution function $\widehat{F}_j(y_j)$, $j = 1, 2$, which may be treated as realizations of uniform random variables u_1 and u_2, respectively. Given $\{\widehat{u}_{1i}, \widehat{u}_{2i}, i = 1, \ldots, N\}$, and a copula, the dependence parameter θ can be estimated as follows:

$$\widehat{\theta}_{\text{TSML}} = \arg\max_{\theta} \sum_{i=1}^{N} \ln c_i(\widehat{u}_{1i}, \widehat{u}_{2i}; \theta).$$

There are two issues to consider. First, the approach is straightforward if the y_j are iid. This may be a reasonable assumption with cross section data, but may be more tenuous in time series applications. Second, because this method of estimating θ uses $\widehat{u}_{1i}, \widehat{u}_{2i}$, which are generated (rather than observed) variates, valid estimation of the variance of $\widehat{\theta}_{\text{TSML}}$ requires going beyond the standard likelihood calculation based on the (Fisher) information matrix.

4.2.2   Parametric sequential approach

Suppose that the appropriate marginal distributions are parametrically specified and are conditioned on covariates. Again we can separate the estimation of marginal and dependence parameters. This approach is computationally attractive if the dimension of θ is large so that the application of FML is problematic. Joint estimation is further encumbered if certain choices of marginal distributions contribute to a flat likelihood function. The method also has an advantage that the specification of the marginals can be tested using diagnostic tests to ensure that they provide an acceptable fit to the data. Appropriate marginals should produce more precise estimates of the dependence parameter.

For the case of continuous random variables, the log likelihood function has the structure given in (4.4). As discussed by Joe (1997), it is often easier to consider the log likelihood of each univariate margin,

$$\mathcal{L}_j(\beta_j) = \sum_{i=1}^{N} \log f_j(y_{ij}|\mathbf{x}_{ij}, \beta_j)$$

and maximize these likelihoods to obtain $\widehat{\beta}_j$ for each margin j. Then treating these values as given, the full likelihood function based on Eq. (4.4) is maximized with respect to only the dependence parameter θ. Following a convention in the statistics literature, Joe refers to this estimation technique as inference functions for margins (IFM).

Under regularity conditions, IFM produces estimates that are consistent with full maximum likelihood (FML), albeit less efficient. Comparing efficiency of IFM and FML is difficult because asymptotic covariance matrices are generally intractable, but for a number of models, IFM may perform favorably compared to ML. However, if efficiency is a concern, then consistent standard errors can be obtained by using the following bootstrap algorithm:

(1) Obtain $\widehat{\beta}_1$, $\widehat{\beta}_2$, and $\widehat{\theta}$ by IFM.
(2) Randomly draw a sample of observations (with replacement) from the data. The randomly drawn sample may be smaller, larger, or the same size as the number of observations in the data.
(3) Using the randomly drawn sample, reestimate β_1, β_2, and θ by IFM and store the values.
(4) Repeat steps (2) and (3) many times and denote each replicated estimate as $\widehat{\beta}_1(r)$, $\widehat{\beta}_2(r)$, and $\widehat{\theta}(r)$ where r is the replication.
(5) Standard errors for parameters $\widehat{\Omega} = (\widehat{\beta}_1, \widehat{\beta}_2, \widehat{\theta})'$ are calculated using the variance matrix $R^{-1} \sum_{r=1}^{R} (\widehat{\Omega}(r) - \widehat{\Omega})(\widehat{\Omega}(r) - \widehat{\Omega})'$ where R is the number of replications.

FML and TSML both produce consistent estimates of the dependence parameter θ. The dependence parameter is often the primary result of interest in empirical applications. For example, in financial studies, portfolio managers are often interested in the joint probability that two or more funds will fail during a recession. In these applications, the dependence parameter indicates correlation between fund performances, and the Fréchet–Hoeffding bounds (discussed in Section 2.1) provide bounds on possible correlation.

4.2.3   Example: Copula-based volatility models

Chen and Fan (2006) consider estimation and model selection of semiparametric copula-based multivariate dynamic (SCOMDY) models. An example of such a model is the generalized autoregressive conditional heteroskedastic (GARCH) model with errors generated by a Gaussian copula or a Student's t-copula. Different choices of the distributions in the copulas generate different nested or non-nested models. The log-likelihood function has a structure similar to (4.4), so Chen and Fan propose a two-step estimator in which the non-copula parameters are estimated first and the copula parameters are estimated conditional on those. Given two or more models estimated in this way, each based on a different copula, a practical issue is how to choose between them. They develop model selection procedures, under the assumption of misspecified copulas, based on a pseudo likelihood ratio (PLR) criterion. Following Vuong (1989) they use the minimum of Kullback–Leibler information criterion (KLIC) over the copulas to measure the closeness of a SCOMDY model to the true model. They establish the asymptotic distribution of the PLR for both the nested and non-nested cases. For non-nested models the PLR criterion has an asymptotic normal distribution and for the nested case it is a mixture of chi-square distributions.

For specificity, consider the example of a GARCH (1,1) with errors from the Gaussian copula. For $j = 1, \ldots, m$

$$y_{jt} = \mathbf{x}'_{jt}\beta_j + \sqrt{h_{jt}}\varepsilon_{jt},$$
$$h_{jt} = k_j + \alpha_j h_{j,t-1} + \delta_j(y_{jt} - \mathbf{x}'_{jt}\beta_j)^2,$$

where $k_j > 0, \alpha_j > 0$, $\delta_j > 0$, and $\alpha_j + \delta_j < 1$. The ε_{jt} are zero mean, unit variance, serially uncorrelated errors generated from a Gaussian copula with covariance matrix $\boldsymbol{\Sigma}$; the covariate vectors are assumed to be exogenous. The estimation procedure of Chen and Fan is ordinary least squares for the parameters β_j and quasi-MLE for $(k_j, \alpha_j, \delta_j)$.

Using $\widehat{}$ to denote sample estimates, let $\widehat{\theta}_j = (\widehat{\beta}_j, \widehat{k}_j, \widehat{\alpha}_j, \widehat{\delta}_j)$ and $\widehat{\theta} = (\widehat{\theta}_1, \ldots, \widehat{\theta}_m)$. Given these estimates, the empirical distribution function of the $\varepsilon_{jt}(\widehat{\theta})$ can be obtained. This is denoted as $\widehat{F}_j(\varepsilon_{jt}(\widehat{\theta}))$, $j = 1, \ldots, m$. At the final stage the likelihood based on a Gaussian copula density $c(\widehat{F}_1(\varepsilon_{1t}(\widehat{\theta})), \ldots, \widehat{F}_m(\varepsilon_{mt}(\widehat{\theta})))$ is maximized to estimate the dependence parameters.

A similar procedure can be applied to estimate GARCH(1,1) models with other copulas. Chen and Fan establish the asymptotic distribution of the dependence parameter and provide an estimation procedure for the variances under possible misspecification of the parametric copula. One interesting result they obtain is that the asymptotic distribution of the dependence parameters is not affected by the estimation of parameters $\widehat{\theta}$.

4.3 Copula Evaluation and Selection

In empirical applications of copulas, one wants to know how well the model fits the data. It is especially useful to know if there are indicators of misspecification. For example, data may exhibit the type of tail dependence that the selected copula cannot capture. Further, if several copulas are tried, one wants to know which one provides the best fit to the data. This section will discuss these practical issues using Monte Carlo experiments for exposition and illustration. We will also present two empirical examples to demonstrate copula estimation of microeconometric models for which parametric joint distributions are not readily available.

4.3.1 Selection criteria

Different copula functions exhibit different dependence patterns. Therefore, if a researcher wants to explore the structure of dependence, he may estimate several copulas and choose one on the basis of best fit to the data. Other methods for choosing copulas are presented in Section 4.5.

The first step in copula estimation is to specify and estimate univariate marginal distributions. This decision should be guided by economic and statistical features of the data. The goodness of fit of the marginal models can and should be evaluated using diagnostic and goodness of fit tests. Many of these will be specific to the parametric form of the marginal model. The better the fit of the marginal, the more precisely we can model the dependence structure. We will illustrate some of these in the section on empirical applications. The second step, potentially more difficult, requires specification of a copula. Here prior information plays a role. For example, if right tail dependence is expected to be a feature of the data, choosing a copula functional form that does not permit such dependence is not appropriate. Choosing a copula that permits only positive dependence is also restrictive if one expects either positive or negative dependence in the relevant data context. Thus, in many empirical settings, choosing a relatively unrestrictive copula is a sensible decision. In many empirical settings trying several copulas to explore the dependence structure is a sound strategy.

The first model selection approach we consider is due to Genest and Rivest (1993) who recommend a technique for choosing among bivariate Archimedean copulas. Assume that two random variables (Y_{1i}, Y_{2i}), $i = 1, \ldots, N$, have a bivariate distribution $F(Y_{1i}, Y_{2i})$ with corresponding copula $C(F_1(Y_1), F_2(Y_2); \theta)$. The researcher must choose the appropriate functional form for $C(\cdot)$ from several available Archimedean copulas. Let the random variable $Z_i = F(Y_{1i}, Y_{2i})$ be described by distribution function $K(z) = \Pr(Z_i \leq z)$. Genest and Rivest show that this distribution function is related to the Archimedean generator function,

$$K(z) = z - \frac{\varphi(z)}{\varphi'(z)}.$$

Identifying the appropriate Archimedean copula is equivalent to identifying the optimal generator function. To determine the appropriate generator:

- Calculate Kendall's tau using the following nonparametric estimator:

$$\widehat{\rho}_\tau = \binom{N}{2}^{-1} \sum_{i<j} \operatorname{sign}\left[(Y_{1i} - Y_{1j})(Y_{2i} - Y_{2j})\right].$$

- Calculate a nonparametric estimate of K by defining the variable

$$Z_i = \{\text{number of } (Y_{1j}, Y_{2j}) \text{ such that } Y_{1j} < Y_{1i}$$
$$\text{and } Y_{2j} < Y_{2i}\}/(N-1)\}$$

for $i = 1, \ldots, N$. Then set $\widehat{K}(z) = $ proportion of Z_i's $\leq z$.

- For φ, a given Archimedean generator, calculate a parametric estimate of K using the equation

$$\widetilde{K}_{\varphi}(z) = z - \frac{\varphi(z)}{\varphi'(z)}.$$

Generators for several popular Archimedean copulas are listed in Table 3.2. Use the nonparametric estimate of τ_n to calculate θ_n in each generator. For each generator function, a different estimate of $\widetilde{K}_{\varphi}(z)$ is obtained. The appropriate generator, and thus the optimal Archimedean copula, is the one for which $\widetilde{K}_{\varphi}(z)$ is closest to the nonparametric estimate $\widehat{K}(z)$. This can be determined by minimizing the distance function $\int (\widetilde{K}_{\varphi}(z) - \widehat{K}(z))^2 dK(z)$.

Ané and Kharoubi (2003) also demonstrate a method for selecting copulas that involves comparing parametric and nonparametric values, but unlike Genest and Rivest, their technique is not limited to the Archimedean class. The idea is to compute a nonparametric empirical copula and compare the values to estimates of parametric copulas. Consider the bivariate case for which an empirical copula $C_e(F_1(Y_1), F_2(Y_2))$ may be calculated as

$$\widehat{C}_e(Y_1, Y_2) = \sum_{i=1}^{N} \sum_{j=1}^{N} \mathbf{1}\{(Y_{j1} \leq Y_{i1}) \text{ and } (Y_{j2} \leq Y_{i2})\}, \qquad (4.9)$$

where $\mathbf{1}\{A\}$ is the indicator function that equals 1 if event A occurs. Next, several parametric copulas are estimated, each denoted $\widetilde{C}_p(F_1(Y_1), F_2(Y_2))$. The parametric copula that is closest to the empirical copula is the most appropriate choice. The researcher may evaluate closeness using a distance estimator, for which a simple example is the sum of squares,

$$\text{Distance} = \sum_{i=1}^{N}(\widehat{C}_{ei} - \widetilde{C}_{pi})^2. \tag{4.10}$$

Ané and Kharoubi (2003) also use distance measures based on the concept of entropy and the Anderson–Darling test, the latter which emphasize deviations in the tails, which is useful for applications in which tail dependence is expected to be important.

4.3.2   Application of model selection to simulated data

As an example, we draw 500 simulated values from a particular copula and calculate $\widehat{C}_e$ and $\widehat{C}_p$ (without explanatory variables, which means only the dependence parameter is estimated for the parametric copulas). For the purpose of demonstration, we compare three copulas with markedly different dependence structures: Clayton, Gumbel, and FGM. The following Table 4.1 reports distance measures based on Eq. (4.10), with asterisks denoting the values for parametric copulas that are closest to the corresponding empirical copula.

For the Clayton DGP, the parametric Clayton copula is closest to the nonparametric empirical copula. Similar results apply for the Gumbel and FGM copulas. This finding is not surprising. Although the distance measure provides a useful ranking of the models in terms of goodness-of-fit, it does not test a hypothesis of model misspecification. While these results attest to the usefulness of empirical copulas in choosing appropriate copulas, approaches which compare empirical and parametric values are currently rarely used in applied microeconometric

Table 4.1 Distance measures for three copulas.

Clayton	Gumbel	FGM
DGP: Clayton with $\theta = 3$		
0.0447*	0.4899	1.8950
DGP: Gumbel with $\theta = 3$		
0.8534	0.1305*	3.2755
DGP: FGM with $\theta = 0.8$		
0.1004	0.0998	0.0415*

Note: The asterisks denote, the values for parametric copular that are closest to the corresponding empirical copula.

applications. The Genest and Rivest method does not consider non-Archimedean copulas such as the Gaussian and FGM copulas, both of which are popular in applied settings. Moreover, the method is computationally more demanding than copula estimation itself. The Ané and Kharoubi technique is also computationally demanding, because one must estimate all copulas under consideration in addition to estimating an empirical copula. If one is already committed to estimate several different parametric copulas, the practitioner might find it easier to forgo nonparametric estimation and instead base copula selection on penalized likelihood criteria discussed below.

As a part of an exploratory analysis of dependence structure, researchers may graphically examine dependence patterns before estimation by plotting the points (Y_{1i}, Y_{2i}); of course, this approach is more appropriate when no covariates are present in the marginal distributions. If the scatter diagram points to a pattern of dependence that is similar to one of the "standard" models, e.g., see the simulated plots in Section 2.5, then this may point to one or more appropriate choices. For example, if Y_1 and Y_2 appear to be highly correlated in the left tail, then Clayton might be an appropriate copula. If dependence appears to be symmetric or negative, then FGM is an appropriate choice, but if dependence is relatively strong, then FGM should be avoided.

In the standard econometric terminology, alternative copula models with a single dependence parameter are said to be non-nested. One approach for choosing between non-nested parametric models estimated by maximum likelihood is to use either the Akaike or (Schwarz) Bayesian information criterion. For example, Bayes information criterion (BIC) is equal to $-2\ln(L) + K\ln(N)$ where $\ln(L)$ is the maximized log likelihood value, K is the number of parameters, and N is the number of observations. Smaller BIC values indicate better fit. However, if all the copulas under consideration have the same K then use of these criteria amounts to choosing the model with the largest likelihood. If, on the other hand there are several specifications of the marginal models with alternative regression structures under consideration, then penalized likelihood criteria are useful for model selection.

In our experience a combination of visual inspection and penalized likelihood measures provides satisfactory guidance in copula selection.

Visual examination of (Y_{1i}, Y_{2i}) provides useful prior indication of choices that are likely to be satisfactory. An example of copula selection is Frees and Valdez (1998) who examine insurance indemnity claims data for which the two variables of interest are indemnity payments and allocated loss adjustment expenses. Using the Genest and Rivest method, they find that the Gumbel copula provides the best fit to the data, although Frank's copula also provides a satisfactory fit. A scatter plot shows that the variables appear to exhibit right tail dependence (Figure 2.1 in their text), which offers further support for the Gumbel copula. Since Clayton copulas exhibit strong left tail dependence, it is not surprising that they find that Clayton provides a poor fit of the data. Finally, they estimate several copulas and find that Gumbel provides the best fit according to an information criterion measure.

4.4   Monte Carlo Illustrations

This section presents Monte Carlo experiments in order to illustrate the effects of copula misspecification. The following two subsections consider cases in which dependent variables are continuous and discrete.

4.4.1   Bivariate normal example

For 500 simulated observations, $i = 1, \ldots, 500$, two normally distributed random variables are generated as

$$y_{1i} = \beta_{11} + \beta_{12}x_{1i} + \eta_{1i},$$
$$y_{2i} = \beta_{12} + \beta_{22}x_{2i} + \eta_{2i},$$

where x_1 and x_2 are independently uniform on $(-0.5, 0.5)$. The terms η_1 and η_2 are jointly distributed standard normal variates drawn from a particular copula with dependence parameter θ using techniques presented in the Appendix.

We estimate five bivariate copulas of the form $C(F_1(y_1|x_1),$ $F_2(y_2|x_2); \theta)$ under the assumption that the marginal distributions F_1 and F_2 are standard normal cdfs,

$$F_j(y_j) = \int \frac{1}{\sigma_j} \phi \left(\frac{y_j - \beta_{j1} - \beta_{j2}x_j}{\sigma_j} \right) dy_j,$$

where $\phi(t) = 1/\sqrt{2\pi}\exp(-t^2/2)$. Each copula is correctly specified; that is, each has the same specification as the corresponding DGP. The objective is to evaluate the properties of the FML estimator applied under the assumption of correct specification of the copula.

The true values for the parameters are: $(\beta_{11}, \beta_{12}, \beta_{21}, \beta_{22}, \sigma_1, \sigma_2) = (2, 1, 0, -0.5, 1, 1)$. The true value of θ for each copula is chosen so that Kendall's tau is approximately equal to 0.3, except for the FGM copula, which cannot accommodate dependence of this magnitude. For the FGM case, θ is set equal to 0.5, which corresponds to a Kendall's tau value of 0.11. The true values of θ are shown in Table 4.2 across the top row. Each Monte Carlo experiment involves 1000 replications. For each replication, new realizations of η_1 and η_2 are randomly drawn which yields new observations y_1 and y_2, but x_1 and x_2 and the true values of the parameters are held constant.

We also show two-way scatter diagrams for the dependent variables using data from one replication of each Monte Carlo experiment. Figure 2.3 is for the case of continuous variables with Gaussian marginals; Figure 4.1 is for the discrete case with Poisson marginals. In all cases, because of the additional variability in the data due to the presence of covariates in the *dgp*, the resulting scatters show higher dispersion than the corresponding ones in Figure 2.3.

The estimation method is full maximum likelihood (FML), which is executed by maximizing the log likelihood function given in Eq. (4.3). The log likelihood function is maximized using a Newton–Ralphson iterative module available in the IML platform of SAS. The module requires the user to specify only the log likelihood function; first derivatives are calculated numerically within the module. For each copula, the Monte Carlo experiment with 1000 replications finished in less than 10 min on a standard desktop machine. However, for larger experiments, the user may wish to provide analytical first derivatives of the log likelihood function, which can greatly reduce estimation times.

For two normally distributed continuous variables, it is unnecessary to estimate a copula function as econometric software can easily estimate Seemingly Unrelated Regression (SUR) models, but specifying the Monte Carlo experiment in terms of normal marginals offers a

Table 4.2 Monte Carlo results for bivariate normal.

	DGP	Clayton ($\theta = 0.86$)		Frank ($\theta = 5.40$)		Gumbel ($\theta = 1.43$)		Gaussian ($\theta = 0.45$)		FGM ($\theta = 0.50$)	
		Mean	St. Dev.	Mean	St. Dev.	Mean	St. Dev.	Mean	St. Dev.	Mean	St. Dev.
β_{11}	2.00	1.999	0.044	1.999	0.041	1.998	0.043	1.999	0.047	1.999	0.044
β_{12}	1.00	1.002	0.133	1.000	0.113	0.999	0.132	1.002	0.133	0.997	0.156
σ_1	1.00	0.998	0.030	0.998	0.031	0.998	0.030	0.996	0.032	0.998	0.032
β_{21}	0.00	-0.001	0.045	-0.001	0.043	-0.001	0.046	0.001	0.044	-0.001	0.046
β_{22}	-0.50	-0.499	0.124	-0.501	0.109	-0.495	0.131	-0.502	0.131	-0.500	0.147
σ_2	1.00	0.997	0.031	0.997	0.031	0.998	0.030	0.997	0.031	0.997	0.033
θ		0.870	0.100	5.429	0.356	1.434	0.055	0.449	0.037	0.504	0.131

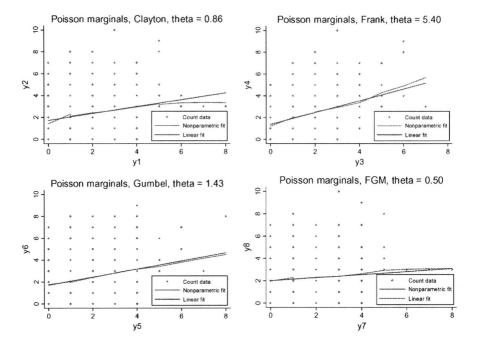

Fig. 4.1 Bivariate simulated data generated with Poisson marginals.

useful frame of reference. Table 4.2 reports the average estimates across replications. The averages of the FML estimates, including estimates of the dependence parameters, are virtually identical to the true values.

An attractive property of copulas is that dependence structures are permitted to be nonlinear. Unfortunately, this also presents difficulties in comparing dependence across different copula functions. Although measures of linear correlation such as Kendall's tau and Spearman's rho may be helpful in cross-copula comparisons, they are not directly comparable because they cannot account for nonlinear dependence structures. The following example illustrates this point.

Data are drawn from the Clayton copula using the same true values for β_{11}, β_{12}, β_{21}, β_{22}, σ_1, and σ_2 that are used in the previous experiment. However, the true value of the dependence parameter is set equal to 4, which corresponds to a Kendall's tau value of 0.67. We then use these simulated data to estimate the Gumbel copula in order

Table 4.3 Monte Carlo results for continuous normal with data drawn from Clayton copula.

	β_{11}	β_{12}	σ_1	β_{21}	β_{22}	σ_2	θ
Mean	2.042	1.000	1.071	0.042	−0.498	1.071	2.510
Std. Dev.	0.045	0.101	0.037	0.044	0.097	0.037	0.132

to determine whether the Gumbel copula is capable of accommodating high degrees of dependence generated from the Clayton copula. A Kendall's tau value of 0.67 translates to a dependence parameter value of 3 for Gumbel's copula. However, at such high levels of correlation, Clayton and Gumbel exhibit different dependence structures, as shown in Section 2.5. As Table 4.3 shows, the Monte Carlo estimates of the Gumbel copula using Clayton data produce a dependence parameter estimate that is smaller than 3.

For highly correlated Clayton variates, most of the dependence is concentrated in the lower tail. However, lower tail dependence is relatively weak for the Gumbel copula. Consequently, it is not surprising that the Gumbel copula is unable to accurately capture dependence generated from a Clayton copula.

The preceding example illustrates that it is difficult to compare dependence parameters across different copulas. To address this complication in interpreting dependence parameters, microeconometric researchers typically estimate several copulas and convert the dependence parameters, post estimation, into Kendall's tau or Spearman's rho. Competing copula families are nonnested so model comparison is not straightforward. Moreover, the dependence parameter in some particular copula family may be estimated to be on the boundary of the parameter space which may make the model comparison problem "irregular." When the competing copula models are "regular" one may use the penalized log-likelihood criterion for model selection and make inferences about dependence based on the "best model." Tail probability properties provide an indicator of another aspect of the dependence structure, which in some applications is of major interest.

4.4.2   Bivariate Poisson example

The next experiment investigates the performance of copula estimation when (y_1, y_2) are discrete random variables. In general, generating discrete variables is more difficult than simulating continuous observations. We adapt the technique of Devroye (1986: 86) presented in the Appendix to simulate two correlated discrete count variables (y_1, y_2). The realizations of (y_1, y_2) are drawn from the copula function $C(F_1(y_1|x_1), F_2(y_2|x_2); \theta)$ where F_1 and F_2 are Poisson distribution functions,

$$F_j(y_{jk}) = \sum_{y=0}^{y_{jk}} \frac{e^{-\mu_j} \mu_j^{y_{jk}}}{y_{jk}!} \qquad \text{for } j = 1, 2$$

where $\mu_j = \exp(\beta_{j1} + \beta_{j2} x_j)$ denotes the conditional mean function, and x_1 and x_2 are independently uniform on $(-0.5, 0.5)$. For each replication, 500 new realizations of (y_1, y_2) are drawn from the copula.

Estimation is by full maximum likelihood (FML) based on the joint probability mass function given in Eq. (4.6). Similar to the experiment using continuous data, the log likelihood function, calculated by Eq. (4.8), is maximized using a Newton–Ralphson iterative procedure in SAS/IML. The Monte Carlo experiments for 1000 replications require similar computation times to the continuous experiments discussed above.

Table 4.4 reports the average estimates across 1000 replications. The true values of the dependence parameters are the same as in the continuous experiment, but the true values of the other parameters are adjusted to ensure that exponential means are not unreasonably large. The true values are: $\beta_{11} = 0.7$; $\beta_{12} = 1.8$; $\beta_{21} = 0.3$; $\beta_{22} = -1.4$. For these true values, the mean values of y_1 and y_2 are 2.01 and 1.35 when calculated at the mean values of x_1 and x_2.

As in the continuous case, averages of FML estimates are virtually identical to the true values. The dependence parameter is slightly more difficult to estimate compared to the continuous example. For example, the true Frank dependence parameter is 5.40, but the average estimate across all replications is 5.46, which means that the simulation misestimates the true value by approximately 1%. Nevertheless, estimates of the dependence parameters are close to their true values.

We experience computational difficulties in estimating the Gaussian copula. Then the experiment was run after applying the continuation transformation (as described in Section 4.1.2 to the generated counts, and replacing the Poisson marginals by normal marginals for $\ln(y_1)$ and $\ln(y_2)$. The results shown in Table 4.4 indicate that the use of the continuation transformation and normal marginals overcomes the computational problem. But the estimates of slope and the dependence are biased. Specifically, the dependence parameter estimate shows an average downward bias of over 35%.

4.5   Empirical Applications

This section applies the copula methodology to three different bivariate applications. The analysis is based on observational, not generated, data. Clearly when working with observational data, there is uncertainty about the DGP, and thus selection of an appropriate copula is an important issue. An appropriate copula is one which best captures dependence features of the outcome variables. It is important to note that some copulas that are popular in applied settings were originally developed for specific empirical applications; for example, the Clayton copula was developed for survival analysis. However, because copulas separate marginal distributions from dependence structures, a copula which might have been motivated by a particular application may still be useful for other applications. For example, the common shock model may have wide applicability for discrete, continuous, and mixed discrete-continuous models. The important consideration when selecting an appropriate copula is whether dependence is accurately represented.

4.5.1   Bivariate Tobit example

The well-known Seemingly Unrelated Regressions (SUR) model is one of the most widely used in econometrics. The key idea is that, except in some special cases, more efficient estimates are obtained by estimating systems of linear equations simultaneously rather than separately if the error terms are jointly related. Most statistical packages include commands to estimate SUR models, especially the linear SUR model and bivariate probit. Nonlinear versions of this model are less often used in empirical work, although efficiency gains from joint estimation

Table 4.4 Monte Carlo results for bivariate poisson.

	DPG	Clayton ($\theta = 0.86$)		Frank ($\theta = 5.40$)		Gumbel ($\theta = 1.43$)		Gauss ($\theta = 0.45$)		FGM ($\theta = 0.50$)	
		Mean	St. Dev.	Mean	St. Dev.	Mean	St. Dev.	Mean	St. Dev.	Mean	St. Dev.
β_{11}	0.70	0.698	0.032	0.698	0.031	0.699	0.033	0.703	0.037	0.698	0.033
β_{12}	1.80	1.801	0.105	1.801	0.086	1.803	0.097	1.714	0.122	1.799	0.111
β_{21}	0.30	0.298	0.042	0.298	0.040	0.300	0.040	0.326	0.044	0.298	0.042
β_{22}	-1.40	-1.399	0.118	-1.401	0.105	-1.397	0.114	-1.227	0.139	-1.399	0.128
θ		0.877	0.119	5.463	0.407	1.437	0.058	0.290	0.047	0.509	0.148

of such models are also to be expected. One variant of the nonlinear SUR model that has been used is the multivariate Tobit model. Such a model is relevant when some variables of interest might be subject to censoring. Although there is an extensive literature on the estimation of univariate Tobit models (Amemiya, 1973, Heckman, 1976, Greene, 1990, Chib, 1992), and the method is widely available in statistical packages, it is less straightforward to estimate a SUR Tobit model. Brown and Lankford (1992) develop a bivariate Tobit model, but their technique is not easily generalized to higher dimensions. Difficulties extending this model to higher dimensions are addressed in Wales and Woodland (1983).[1]

In this section, we demonstrate how copula functions are used to estimate a SUR Tobit model with relative ease. The copula approach offers several advantages over existing techniques. First, the researcher may consider models with wide ranges of dependence that are not feasible under the Brown and Lankford (1992) bivariate normal specification. Second, the model can be extended to three or more jointly related censored outcomes using the techniques presented in Section 3.5. These higher dimensional models can be estimated using conventional maximum likelihood approaches and do not require Monte Carlo integration or Bayesian techniques.

For a sample of observations $i = 1, \ldots, N$, consider two continuous latent variables y_1^* and y_2^* which are specified as

$$y_{ij}^* = \mathbf{x}_{ij}' \boldsymbol{\beta}_j + \varepsilon_{ij} \quad \text{for } j = 1, 2.$$

If $y_{ij}^* > 0$, then the variable y_{ij} is observed, but if $y_{ij}^* \leq 0$, then $y_{ij} = 0$. If ε_{ij} are normally distributed as $\mathcal{N}(0, \sigma^2)$, then the density function of y_{ij} is

$$f_j(y_{ij} | \boldsymbol{\beta}_j' \mathbf{x}_{ij}) = \prod_{y_{ij}=0} \left[1 - \Phi\left(\frac{\mathbf{x}_{ij}' \boldsymbol{\beta}_j}{\sigma_j} \right) \right] \prod_{y_{ij}>0} \phi\left(\frac{y_{ij} - \mathbf{x}_{ij}' \boldsymbol{\beta}_j}{\sigma_j} \right),$$

---

[1] Huang et al. (1987), Meng and Rubin (1996), Huang (1999), and Kamakura and Wedel (2001) develop estimation procedures for SUR Tobit models. However, all of these approaches are computationally demanding and difficult to implement, which may partially explain why the SUR Tobit model has not been used in many empirical applications.

and the corresponding cdf $F_j(y_{ij}|\beta'_j\mathbf{x}_{ij})$ is obtained by replacing $\phi(\cdot)$ with $\Phi(\cdot)$ in the second part of the expression.[2] A bivariate Tobit representation can be expressed using a copula function. For the censored outcomes y_{i1} and y_{i2}, a SUR bivariate Tobit distribution is given by

$$F(y_1, y_2) = C\left(F_1(y_{i1}|\mathbf{x}'_{i1}\beta_1), F_2(y_{i2}|\mathbf{x}'_{i2}\beta_2); \theta\right).$$

The log likelihood function is calculated as shown in Eq. (4.3), and the estimated values are obtained using a Newton–Ralphson iterative procedure in SAS/IML. Any econometric package that accommodates user-defined likelihood functions, such as STATA or LIMDEP, could also be used to estimate the model. As with conventional maximum likelihood models, standard errors may be calculated from the likelihood Hessian or outer-product of likelihood gradients. Standard errors reported below were estimated using the robust sandwich formula based on these two matrices. Our optimization procedure in SAS/IML did not require analytical first derivatives of the log likelihood function, but providing them might improve estimation efficiency, especially for large data sets. For the application presented below, the models converged in less than 2 min on a standard desktop machine without specifying first derivatives.

We apply a copula-based SUR Tobit to model the relationship between out-of-pocket (SLFEXP) and non-out-of-pocket medical expenses (NONSLF) of elderly Americans, using 3206 cross-section observations from the year 2000 Health and Retirement Survey (HRS). Approximately 12% of these individuals reports zero out-of-pocket expenses, and approximately 20% reports zero non-out-of-pocket expenses. The outcome variables are rescaled as follows: $y_1 = \log(\text{SLFEXP}+1)$ and $y_2 = \log(\text{NONSLF}+1)$.

Control variables are supplemental insurance, age, race, gender, education, income, marital status, measures of self-reported health, and spousal information.[3] We include the same explanatory variables in

---

[2] It is important to note that Tobit models of this form rely on correct specification of the error term ε. Heteroskedasticity or nonnormality lead to inconsistency.

[3] We treat insurance status as exogenous, although there is a case for treating it as endogenous because insurance is often purchased in anticipation of future health care needs. Treating endogeneity would add a further layer of complexity to the model.

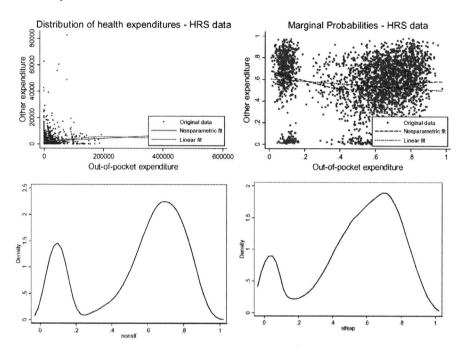

Fig. 4.2 HRS expenditure example.

both $\mathbf{x}'_{i1}$ and $\mathbf{x}'_{i2}$, although the two sets of covariates need not be identical. Even after conditioning on these variables, the two measures of medical expenses are expected to be correlated. The potential source of dependence is unmeasured factors such as negative health shocks that might increase all types of medical spending, attitudes to health risks, and choice of life style. On the other hand, having supplementary insurance may reduce out-of-pocket costs (SLFEXP) and raise insurance reimbursements (NONSLF). Therefore, it is not clear a priori whether the dependence is positive or negative.

To explore the dependence structure and the choice of the appropriate copula, Figure 4.2 plots the pairs (y_1, y_2). The variables appear to exhibit negative dependence in which individuals with high SLF-EXP (out-of-pocket) expenses report low NONSLF (non-out-of-pocket) expenses, and vice versa. Therefore, copulas that do not permit negative dependence, such as Clayton and Gumbel, might be inappropriate.

Beyond the slight indication of negative dependence, the scatter graph does not provide much guidance in the choice of an appropriate copula. It is important to note, however, that the model above measures dependence after controlling for explanatory variables. Consequently, dependence conditional on covariates might be different than unconditional dependence. A valid empirical approach is to estimate several different copulas and choose the model that yields the largest penalized log-likelihood value.

Another exploratory technique is to estimate the marginal models, calculate the cumulative marginal probabilities, and generate a two-way scatter plot. One can also examine the kernel density plots of the marginal probabilities. The top right panel in Figure 4.2 provides this information. The scatter plot of the marginal probabilities reveals 3 or 4 clusters of observations. Two of these clusters are quite sizeable, while the remaining two are much smaller. One interpretation is that the clusters suggest a mixture specification. A two- or three-component finite mixture of copulas may provide a better fit than any single copula; within each mixture component, roughly corresponding to a cluster of observations, the dependence structure may be different. The bimodal pattern of individual marginal probabilities, revealed by the kernel density plots, is also consistent with a mixture formulation. While finite mixture copulas have been used in Hu (2004) and Chen and Fan (2006), their use in regression contexts is not yet widespread, so we do not pursue this issue here.

Table 4.5 shows bivariate Tobit results for four copulas: Clayton, Gaussian, Frank, and FGM. Although there is some variation, the estimates of coefficients are quite similar across the four copulas and consistent with expectations. Therefore, for brevity the table reports only estimates of the dependence parameter θ. Estimates of the Gaussian, Frank, and FGM copulas indicate that dependence is negative, with the Gaussian copula attaining the highest likelihood value. Because the Clayton and Gumbel copulas do not permit negative dependence, we experience computational problems in the estimation algorithm. The Clayton estimate of the dependence parameter settles on the lower bound of its permissible range (0.001), and the Gumbel model fails to converge to any value. The fact that these two copulas fail to con-

Table 4.5 Results for bivariate Tobit.

	Clayton		Gaussian		Frank		FGM	
	Estimate	St. Err.	Estimate	St. Err.	Estimate	St. Err.	Estimate	St. Err.
θ (TSML)	0.001**	0.0001	−0.166**	0.028	−0.741**	0.197	−0.322**	0.072
θ (TSML)	0.001	0.028	−0.159**	0.025	−0.665**	0.146	−0.266**	0.061
log-like (FML)	−4024.96		−15552.08		−15555.35		−15560.73	

verge can be interpreted as further evidence of misspecification that stems from using copulas that do not support negative dependence. This example also indicates computational difficulties one might experience when using a misspecified copula.

The second from the last row of Table 4.5 presents estimates of θ based on two-step maximum likelihood (TSML) in which the estimates of the marginal models are used to generate probabilities that are then substituted into a copula which is then used to estimate only the dependence parameter. In this application both steps are parametric. The results for the estimated dependence parameter are similar to those based on the full maximum likelihood (FML) procedure. An exception is the result for the Gumbel copula for which the estimation algorithm did not converge under full maximum likelihood. Under TSML, however, the estimated value of θ is 1.031 (0.027), which is close to the boundary value of 1.0. These results suggest that TSML is not only a convenient estimation method, but it may also avoid some of the computational problems of FML under misspecification. When, however, the dependence parameter settles at a boundary value, misspecification should be suspected.

This example illustrates how models that were previously challenging to estimate using established methods can be handled with relative ease using the copula approach. Without copulas, the only available methods for estimating SUR Tobit models would involve complicated simulation-based algorithms. In contrast, using copula methods, the joint distribution can be expressed as a function of the marginals, and estimation proceeds by standard maximum likelihood techniques.

4.5.2   Bivariate negative binomial example

Our second application is a bivariate model for discrete (count) data with negative binomial marginals. The application is a model of the number of prescribed and non-prescribed medications taken by individuals over a two-week period obtained from the Australian Health Survey 1977–1978. The data and an early analysis based on the negative binomial regression are in Cameron et al. (1988). Outside of the bivariate probit model, there are few, if any, bivariate representations of jointly dependent discrete variables. This reflects the fact that multivariate distributions of discrete outcomes often do not have closed form expressions, unless the dependence structure is restricted in some special way. Munkin and Trivedi (1999) discuss difficulties associated with bivariate count models. Extending an earlier model of Marshall and Olkin (1990), they propose an alternative bivariate count model with a flexible dependence structure, but their estimation procedure relies on Monte Carlo integration and is computationally demanding, especially for large samples.

We consider two measures of drug use that are possibly dependent: prescription and non-prescription medicines. Although it is reasonable to assume that these two variables are correlated, it is not clear whether dependence is positive or negative, because in some cases the two may be complements and in some cases substitutes. A 64 degrees-of-freedom chi-square contingency test of association has a p-value of 0.82; about 58% of sample respondents record a zero frequency for both variables.

Let prescription and non-prescription medicines be denoted y_1 and y_2, respectively. We assume negative binomial-2 (NB2) marginals (as Cameron et al. (1988) showed that this specification fits the data well):

$$f_j(y_{ji}|\mathbf{x}'_{ij}\boldsymbol{\beta}_j, \psi_j) = \frac{\Gamma(y_{ji} + \psi_j^{-1})}{\Gamma(y_{ji} + 1)\Gamma(\psi_j^{-1})} \left(\frac{\psi_j^{-1}}{\psi_j^{-1} + \xi_{ij}} \right)^{\psi_j^{-1}} \left(\frac{\xi_{ij}}{\psi_j^{-1} + \xi_{ij}} \right)^{y_{ji}}$$
$$\text{for } j = 1, 2, \tag{4.11}$$

where $\xi_{ij} = \exp(\mathbf{x}'_{ij}\boldsymbol{\beta}_j)$ is the conditional mean, and the conditional variance is $\text{var}[y_{ij}|\cdot] = \xi_{ij} + \psi_j\xi_{ij}^2$, where ψ_j is the overdispersion parameter. The corresponding cdf is calculated as

$$F_j(y_{ji}|\mathbf{x}'_{ij}\boldsymbol{\beta}_j, \psi_j) = \sum_{y_{ji}=0}^{y_{ji}} f_j(y_{ji}|\mathbf{x}'_{ij}\boldsymbol{\beta}_j, \psi_j).$$

After the marginal distributions are specified, the joint distribution of prescription and non-prescription drugs is obtained by plugging the NB2 marginals into a copula function,

$$F(y_1, y_2) = C\left(F_1(y_1|\mathbf{x}'_{i2}\boldsymbol{\beta}_2, \psi_1), F_2(y_2|\mathbf{x}'_{i2}\boldsymbol{\beta}_2, \psi_2); \theta \right).$$

The copula log likelihood function is calculated by taking differences as shown in Eq. (4.6), and the estimated values are obtained by maximum likelihood methods as previously discussed.

The data consist of 5190 observations of single-person households from the Australian National Survey 1977–1978. See Cameron et al. (1988) for a detailed description of the data. Explanatory variables include age, gender, income, and five variables related to health status and chronic conditions. Three insurance variables indicate whether the individual is covered by supplementary private insurance and whether public insurance is provided free of charge. For drug use, plotting the (y_1, y_2) pairs of counts is not informative in choosing an appropriate copula function. In part this is due to a large number of tied $(y_1 = y_2)$ values. There are 2451 ties, the overwhelming majority (2431) at 0 and 1. If the continuation transformation is applied by adding independent pseudo random uniform $(0, 1)$ draws to both y_1 and y_2, then the scatter diagram appears to indicate negative dependence. In the absence of a clear indication of how to proceed, a sensible approach is to estimate several different copulas and compare converged likelihood values.

As Table 4.6 reveals, Clayton and Gumbel both encounter convergence problems similar to those in the previous empirical example. Recall that these copulas are only suitable for modeling positive dependence. The Gaussian copula also encounters convergence difficulties, as is evident by its fitted estimated likelihood, which is considerably lower than that for the FGM copula. Copulas with weaker tail dependence, such as the Frank and FGM, seem to perform better. This suggests weak negative dependence, because whereas FGM provides a satisfactory fit, it only accommodates modest amount of dependence. The two copulas that provide the best fit are Frank and FGM. Estimates of β_1, β_2 (not reported in the table) are robust across the Frank and FGM copulas. These results show the importance of selecting copulas appropriate for given data. Failure of the estimation algorithm could be an indication of mismatch (inconsistency) between the properties of the data and the copula restriction on the dependence parameter.

For the three specifications which could not be estimated because of convergence problems, we repeated the exercise after making two

Table 4.6 Results for copula model with negative binomial marginals.

	Clayton		Gumbel		Gaussian		Frank		FGM	
	Estimate	St. Err	Estimate	St. Err	Estimate	St. Err	Estimate	St. Err	Estimate	St. Err
θ (FML-NB)	0.001	0.0004	2.226**	0.042	0.956**	0.001	−0.966**	0.108	−0.449**	0.062
θ (TSML-NB)	0.001	0.004	2.427	0.061	0.949	0.001	−0.960	0.148	−0.446	0.058
θ (FML-Poisson)	no conv.		no conv.		no conv.		−0.414	0.051	−0.407	0.034
log-like (FML-NB)	−9389.32		−13348.41		−16899.43		−9347.84		−9349.11	
θ (FML-Normal)	0.000	0.009	1.001	0.014	−0.0595	0.014	—		—	
log-like (FML-Normal)	−15361.38		−15361.48		−15352.51		—		—	

changes. First the original count data were replaced by continued data obtained by adding uniform (0,1) random draws. This transformation reduces the incidence of ties in the data. Second, we replaced the negative binomial marginals by normal marginals, but with the same conditional mean specification. These changes made it possible to estimate the Gaussian copula; the estimated dependence parameter is -0.0595. The estimation of Clayton and Gumbel copulas again failed with the dependence parameter settling at the boundary values. These estimates at boundary values are not valid maximum likelihood estimates.

Next we consider the effects of misspecifying the marginals. If the marginals are in the linear exponential family, misspecification of either the conditional mean or the variance will affect inference about dependence. In the present example, negative binomial marginals fit the data significantly better than Poisson marginals due to overdispersion, see Table IV in Cameron et al. (1988). Further, in a bivariate model there is potential for confounding overdispersion and dependence, see Munkin and Trivedi (1999).

We also estimated the copulas under Poisson marginals using both the FML and TSML methods. The estimation algorithms for FML and TSML failed to converge for the Clayton, Gumbel, and Gaussian copulas. Given the analysis of the foregoing paragraphs, this result is not a surprise – Clayton and Gumbel copulas do not support negative dependence that is implied by the Frank and FGM copulas, for which more satisfactory results were obtained. Under Poisson marginals, however, convergence of the optimization algorithm was fragile for the Frank copula, but was achieved for the FGM specification, which produced results similar to those for the case of negative binomial marginals; see Table 4.6, second from last row. Thus in the FGM case, where the copula model was computationally tractable, the neglect of overdispersion did not appear to affect the estimates of the dependence parameter. But in the case of Frank copula, the dependence parameter estimated under Poisson marginals was less than half the value estimated under negative binomial marginals.

Our results suggest that in estimating copulas – especially the Gaussian copula – for discrete variables there may be some advantage in analyzing "continued data" rather than discrete data. Applying the continuation transformation introduces measurement error and this will introduce some bias in the results, which may be substantial if the range of data is limited. When the data are inconsistent with the restrictions on the range of dependence parameter, this may be indicated by the failure of the convergence of maximum likelihood algorithm or by estimated value of the dependence parameter settling at the boundary of the admissible interval. There is a role for specification tests of dependence based on marginals.

4.5.3   Co-movement of commodity prices example

Modeling the joint behavior of asset or commodity prices is one of the most common applications of copulas. Whereas we have mainly used copulas in microeconometric settings, we next present an example of how copulas may be used to model co-movement of prices in a financial time series setting. The example draws on Deb et al. (1996) which used multivariate GARCH models to test a variety of hypotheses about the co-movements in prices of largely "unrelated" commodities. As the authors made clear, that text concentrated mainly on linear dependence measures, and found relatively limited evidence in support of the hypothesis that herd like behavior in financial markets may account for dependence between price changes of commodities that are essentially unrelated in either consumption or production. Here we revisit the issue using the copula methodology which permits us to test the hypothesis of asymmetric or tail dependence. Unlike the Deb et al. (1996) study we shall only report results for one pair of prices because our interest in this example is only illustrative.

We consider monthly commodity price data from 1974–1992 of maize and wheat. Let Δy_{1t} and Δy_{2t} denote the first-difference of the log of U.S. prices of maize and wheat, respectively. The time series characteristics of these variables are as follows. Maize prices are more volatile than wheat prices; the average monthly percentage change is 7.6% for maize and 4.9% for wheat. The range of variation is $(-22\%, +29\%)$ for maize and $(-18\%, 25\%)$ for wheat. Both time series display strong excess kurtosis and the joint test of zero skewness and excess kurtosis is easily rejected. The evidence on serial correlation in each time series is somewhat ambiguous. The Ljung-Box portmanteau test of zero serial correlation is rejected if the test is based on 13 leading autocorrelation coefficients, but not if we use 40 coefficients. The null hypothesis of no ARCH effects is not rejected at the 5% and 10% significance if we consider the first three lags only. These features of our data suggest that copula estimation is a reasonable exercise for these data.

The joint distribution of these prices is specified using a copula function, $C(F_1(\Delta y_{1t}), F_2(\Delta y_{2t}); \theta)$. In view of the observed excess kurtosis in both time series, we assume that the marginal distributions follow Student's t-distribution with 5 degrees of freedom.[4] In preliminary analysis, macroeconomic variables such as inflation, money supply, and exchange rates had minimal effects on the prices of these commodities, and therefore, the marginal distributions are estimated without explanatory variables. Under this specification, the dependence parameter θ indicates whether changes in the prices of maize and wheat are dependent over time.

The top two panels of Figure 4.3 show the two time series, Δy_{1t} and Δy_{2t}; their scatter plot is shown in the left panel in the bottom row. The scatter plot is suggestive of positive dependence, and slightly more points appear to lie northeast of the $(0,0)$ origin. This is somewhat indicative of upper tail dependence, although the graph does not provide conclusive evidence. The bottom right panel shows the scatter plot of the residuals from autoregression of Δy_{jt} on $\Delta y_{j,t-1}$ and $\Delta y_{j,t-2}$, $j = 1, 2$. Comparison of the two bottom panels shows that the two scatter plots look similar.

Table 4.7 shows estimates of dependence parameters and log likelihood values for several copulas. The first row shows results based on univariate marginals. Four of the five copulas reveal significant positive dependence in commodity prices, while the dependence parameter for the Clayton copula settles on the lower bound of its permissible range (0.001). The Gumbel copula produces the largest maximized likelihood value, which indicates that changes in maize and wheat prices exhibit upper tail dependence. That is, months in which there are large

---

[4] The t-distribution allows for more mass in the tails compared to the more commonly used normal distribution, and 5 degrees of freedom assures the existence of the first 4 moments.

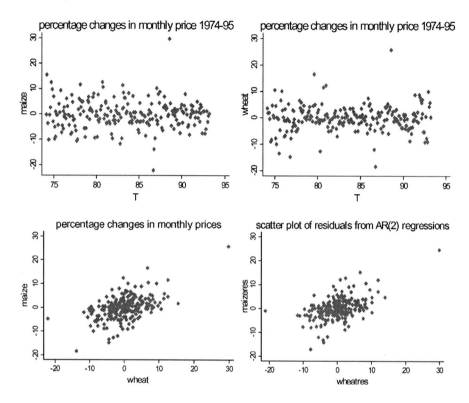

Fig. 4.3 Comovements in wheat and maize price changes.

increases in maize prices also tend to have large increases in wheat prices. This would be plausible if both crops are produced in regions affected by similar weather patterns. The fact that maximum likelihood estimation of the Clayton copula fails to converge indicates that price changes in maize and wheat do not exhibit substantial lower tail dependence.

We repeated our calculations first by including covariates as in Deb et al. (1996), and then also under the assumption that the marginal distributions are Student's t with 3 degrees of freedom. These results are qualitatively similar to those mentioned above. A deeper study of co-movements using copula methods may yield further useful insights.

Because the tests of serial correlation suggest that both price series are serially correlated, we repeated the estimation exercise using, for

Table 4.7 Dependence parameter estimates for maize and wheat comovements.

	Clayton		Gumbel		Gaussian		Frank		FGM	
	Estimate	St. Err	Estimate	St. Err	Estimate	St. Err	Estimate	St. Err	Estimate	St. Err
θ (FML)	0.001	0.026	1.144**	0.027	0.260**	0.033	1.914**	0.360	0.520**	0.085
θ (TSML–AR2)	0.001	0.027	1.137**	0.025	0.247**	0.034	1.713**	0.343	0.488**	0.087
log-like (FML)	−980.64		−1922.31		−1940.37		−1982.48		−1994.25	

each time series, "pre-whitened" residuals from a second order autoregression for each series. These residuals were used in a two-step procedure similar to that of Chen and Fan (2006) mentioned earlier. These results are shown in the second row of Table 4.7. Once again, the previous conclusions about dependence, and especially upper tail dependence are confirmed.

In many applied time series studies, the assumption of joint normality is restrictive but fairly common. In contrast, by estimating several different copulas with varying dependence patterns, one can potentially gain a more detailed understanding of how commodity prices are related.

There are other settings in which the copula based modeling of comovements has been a fruitful alternative. For example, Heinen and Rengifo (2003a, 2003b) consider analyzing comovements between counts in a time series setting. As demonstrated in Cameron and Trivedi (1998) discrete time series modeling is quite awkward, and that of its multivariate variants is even more so. Then copula based time series modeling is potentially a very useful alternative specification.

4.6   Causal Modeling and Latent Factors

The causal effect of one variable on another is often of particular interest in econometric modeling. In the copula framework, when the causal effect concerns an exogenous variable, estimation is straightforward, as the marginal distributions can be parameterized by functions of explanatory variables. However, complications arise when the researcher's interest lies in conditional statements such as $\Pr[u_1|u_2]$ rather than $\Pr[u_1, u_2]$, as the arguments in copula functions are *marginal* as opposed to *conditional* distributions.

This section briefly discusses conditional modeling using copulas and provides an example based on the bivariate sample selection model. This is followed by discussion of a closely related alternative to copula modeling that has appeared in the literature, the latent factor model.

4.6.1   Conditional copulas

For continuous random variables, a straightforward method for recovering the conditional distribution, given the joint distribution, is to differentiate as follows:

$$C_{U_1|U_2}(u_1, u_2) = \frac{\partial C(u_1, u_2)}{\partial u_2},$$
$$C_{U_2|U_1}(u_1, u_2) = \frac{\partial C(u_1, u_2)}{\partial u_1}. \tag{4.12}$$

For copulas with complicated parametric forms, differentiating might be awkward. Zimmer and Trivedi (2006) demonstrate that Bayes' Rule can also be used to recover conditional copula as follows:

$$C_{U_1|U_2}(u_1, u_2) = \frac{C(u_1, u_2)}{u_2}.$$

Similarly, survival copulas are useful because the conditional probability $\Pr[U_1 > u_1 \mid U_2 > u_2]$ can be expressed via survival copulas:

$$\Pr[U_1 > u_1 \mid U_2 > u_2] = \frac{1 - u_1 - u_2 + C(u_1, u_2)}{1 - u_2} = \frac{\overline{C}(1 - u_1, 1 - u_2)}{1 - u_2}. \tag{4.13}$$

At the time of this writing, examples of conditional modeling using copulas are relatively rare in econometrics. The following example is one such application.

4.6.2 Copula-based bivariate sample selection example

The bivariate sample selection model has been extensively used in economics and other social sciences. There are a number of variants, one of which has the following structure.

The model has two continuous latent variables with marginal distribution functions $F_j(y_j^*) = \Pr[Y_j^* \leq y_j]$, $j = 1, 2$, and joint distribution $F(y_1^*, y_2^*) = \Pr[Y_1^* \leq y_1^*, Y_2^* \leq y_2^*]$. Let y_2^* denote the outcome of interest, which is observed only if $y_1^* > 0$. For example, y_1^* determines whether to participate in the labor market and y_2^* determines how many hours to work. The **bivariate sample selection model** consists of a **selection equation** such that

$$y_1 = 1[y_1^* > 0] \tag{4.14}$$

and an **outcome equation** such that

$$y_2 = 1[y_1^* > 0]y_2^*. \tag{4.15}$$

That is, y_2 is observed when $y_1^* > 0$ but not when $y_1^* \le 0$. One commonly used variant of this model specifies a linear model with additive errors for the latent variables,

$$y_1^* = \mathbf{x}_1' \beta_1 + \varepsilon_1 \tag{4.16}$$
$$y_2^* = \mathbf{x}_2' \beta_2 + \varepsilon_2.$$

Suppose that the bivariate distribution of $(\varepsilon_1\ \varepsilon_2)$ is parametrically specified, e.g., bivariate normal. The bivariate sample selection model therefore has likelihood function

$$L = \prod_{i=1}^{N} \{\Pr[y_{1i}^* \le 0]\}^{1-y_{1i}} \left\{ f_{2|1}(y_{2i} \mid y_{1i}^* > 0) \times \Pr[y_{1i}^* > 0] \right\}^{y_{1i}}, \tag{4.17}$$

where the first term is the contribution when $y_{1i}^* \le 0$, since then $y_{1i} = 0$, and the second term is the contribution when $y_{1i}^* > 0$. This likelihood function is general and can be specialized to linear or nonlinear models. The case of bivariate normality is well known in econometrics literature; for details see, for example, Amemiya (1985: 385–387).

The presence of the conditional distribution $f_{2|1}(y_{2i} \mid y_{1i}^* > 0)$ in the likelihood presents complications in estimation, and thus conditional copulas calculated by Eq. (4.12) might be useful. Heckman's model (1976) assumes a joint normal distribution. On the other hand, Lee (1983) shows that the Gaussian copula can be used to relax the assumption that the marginal distributions are normal, but he never explicitly mentioned copulas. Lee's idea was slow to gain acceptance, but recent texts by Prieger (2002) and Genius and Strazzera (2004) have relaxed the assumptions of marginal and joint normality. Smith (2003) provides a general copula-based framework for this model by demonstrating that copulas can be used to extend the standard analysis to any bivariate distribution with given marginals.

First, observe that the conditional density can be written as follows in terms of marginal densities and distribution functions:

$$f_{2|1}(y_2 | Y_1^* > 0) = (1 - F_1(0))^{-1} \frac{\partial}{\partial y_2} [F_2(y_2) - F(0, y_2)]$$

$$= (1 - F_1(0))^{-1} \left(f_2(y_2) - \frac{\partial}{\partial y_2} [F_2(y_2)] \right),$$

where $f_2(y_2) = \partial[F_2(y_2)]/\partial y_2$, which after substitution into (4.17) yields

$$L = \prod_{i=1}^{N} [F_1(0)]^{1-y_{1i}} [f_2(y_{2i}) - \frac{\partial}{\partial y_2}[F(0, y_{2i})].$$ (4.18)

Once the likelihood is written in this form it is immediately obvious, as pointed out by Smith (2003), that we can generate analytical expressions for the otherwise awkward-to-handle term $\partial[F(0, y_{2i})]/\partial y_2$ in the likelihood using alternative specifications of copulas. For the bivariate Archimedean class of copulas $C(F_1(y_1), F_2(y_2); \theta)$, with the generator φ and dependence parameter θ, this term simplifies to

$$\frac{\partial[F(0, y_2)]}{\partial y_2} = \frac{\varphi'(F_2)}{\varphi'(C_\theta)} \times f_2.$$ (4.19)

Smith (2003) provides an empirical analysis using eight different copulas. Moreover, he extends the copula-based selection model to other variants, including the so-called "Roy model" (also called the "regimes model"); see also Smith (2005). Smith's extension of the bivariate normal selection model provides an important extension of the methods available in the literature. The approach can also be used to model selection in the context of discrete outcomes, e.g., event counts.

4.6.3 Copulas and latent factor models

We now consider another approach to modeling dependence in the context of nonlinear regression models that arise in the context of analysis of cross section survival data, event counts, jointly dependent continuous and discrete variables and so forth. Latent factors have been used to model conditional dependence, but they can also be viewed as a general approach to joint modeling.

The latent factor approach that is considered has an important similarity with the copula approach in that the joint model is built using marginal (regression) models in which either common or correlated latent factors enter the models in the same manner as regressors. Their simultaneous presence in different marginals generates dependence between variables. Such latent factor models have a long history in statistics. In the context of bivariate distributions they have appeared under a variety of names such as the shared frailty model in survival analysis (Hougaard, 2000), trivariate reduction model and latent factor models (Skrondal and Rabe-Hesketh, 2004). Generically they are all mixture models and can also be interpreted as random effects models, the difference being due to the structure placed on the way the random effects are introduced into the model and the implicit restrictions that are imposed on the dependence structure.

In choosing a statistical framework for modeling dependence, the structure of dependence should be carefully considered. In the context of regression, common observable variables in regression functions usually account for some dependence. However, models may specify additional dependence through common unobserved factors, usually referred to as "frailty" in demography and "unobserved heterogeneity" in econometrics. Dependence induced by such factors can follow a variety of structures. Hougaard (2000) discusses dependence in multivariate survival models under the headings of common events and common risks. In survival models random shocks may induce dependence only for short durations or only for long durations. In bivariate event count models dependence may be induced for low counts or high counts, and not necessarily all counts. In longitudinal data models dependence may be induced by persistent or transient random factors. Thus, how to model dependence is not an issue that will elicit a mechanical response.

Marshall–Olkin Example. We now consider some specific examples. Marshall and Olkin (1990) generate bivariate distributions from mixtures and convolutions of product families in a manner analogous to Eq. (3.6). Consider the bivariate distribution

$$f(y_1, y_2 | x_1, x_2) = \int_0^\infty f_1(y_1 | x_1, \nu) f_2(y_2 | x_2, \nu) g(\nu) d\nu, \qquad (4.20)$$

where f_1, f_2, and g are univariate densities, and $\nu > 0$, may be interpreted as common unobserved heterogeneity affecting both counts. Let $f_1(y_1 | x_1, \nu)$ and $f_2(y_2 | x_2, \nu)$ denote negative binomial marginal distributions for counted variables y_1 and y_2, with conditional means $\mu_1 | \nu = \exp(x_1 \beta_1 + \nu)$ and $\mu_2 | \nu = \exp(x_2 \beta_2 + \nu)$. Thus, a bivariate negative binomial mixture generated in this way will have univariate negative binomial mixtures. This approach suggests a way of specifying or justifying overdispersed and correlated count models, based on a suitable choice of $g(.)$, more general than in the example given above. Marshall and Olkin (1990) generate a bivariate negative binomial assuming that ν has gamma distribution with parameter α^{-1}. That is,

$$
\begin{aligned}
h(y_1, y_2 | \alpha^{-1}) &= \int_0^\infty \left[(\mu_1 \nu)^{y_1} \exp(-\mu_1 \nu)/y_1!\right] \left[(\mu_2 \nu)^{y_2} \exp(-\mu_2 \nu)/y_2!\right] \\
&\quad \times \left[\nu^{\alpha^{-1}-1} \exp(-\nu)/\Gamma(\alpha^{-1})\right] d\nu \\
&= \frac{\Gamma(y_1 + y_2 + \alpha^{-1})}{y_1! y_2! \Gamma(\alpha^{-1})} \left[\frac{\mu_1}{\mu_1 + \mu_2 + 1}\right]^{y_1} \left[\frac{\mu_2}{\mu_1 + \mu_2 + 1}\right]^{y_2} \\
&\quad \times \left[\frac{1}{\mu_1 + \mu_2 + 1}\right]^{\alpha^{-1}}.
\end{aligned} \tag{4.21}
$$

This model is straightforward to estimate by maximum likelihood. However, because the model restricts the unobserved heterogeneity to the identical component for both count variables, the correlation between the two count variables,

$$
\text{Corr}(y_1, y_2) = \frac{\mu_1 \mu_2}{\sqrt{(\mu_1^2 + \alpha \mu_1)(\mu_2^2 + \alpha \mu_2)}}, \tag{4.22}
$$

must be positive. The model can only accommodate positive dependence. Note further that α does double duty as it is the overdispersion parameter and partly determines correlation.

Consider whether a more flexible dependence structure could be introduced here. More flexible bivariate and multivariate parametric count data models can be constructed by introducing correlated, rather than identical, unobserved heterogeneity components in models. For example, suppose y_1 and y_2 are, respectively, $Poisson(\mu_1 | \nu_1)$ and $Poisson(\mu_2 | \nu_2)$

$$
\mu_1 | \mathbf{x}, \nu_1 = \exp(\beta_{01} + \lambda_1 \nu_1 + \mathbf{x}_1' \boldsymbol{\beta}_1), \tag{4.23}
$$

and

$$
\mu_2 | \mathbf{x}, \nu_2 = \exp(\beta_{02} + \lambda_2 \nu_2 + \mathbf{x}_2' \boldsymbol{\beta}_2), \tag{4.24}
$$

where ν_1 and ν_2 represent correlated unobserved heterogeneity. Dependence between y_1 and y_2 is induced if ν_1 and ν_2 are correlated. We refer to (ν_1, ν_2) as latent factors, and to (λ_1, λ_2) as factor loadings. For example, we could assume (ν_1, ν_2) to be bivariate normal distributed with correlation ρ. However, maximum likelihood estimation of $(\beta_{01}, \beta_1, \beta_{02}, \beta_2)$ is not straight-forward for several reasons. First, because (ν_1, ν_2) are latent factors, we need to fix the location and scale, and introduce normalizations that allow identification of the factor loadings. The usual solution is to fix the mean to equal 0, the variance to be 1, and one of the factor loadings, λ_1 or λ_2, to equal 1, and to leave the other as a free parameter, which determines the correlation between the latent factors. Second, under the assumption of normality there is no analytical form for the integral as was the case in Eq. (4.21), so maximum simulated likelihood (MSL), rather than standard maximum likelihood is required. MSL estimation of such models requires numerically intensive methods, such as numerical or Monte Carlo integration, see Munkin and Trivedi (1999). In applying MSL, each term in the likelihood is of the form:

$$f(y_1, y_2 | \mathbf{x}_1, \mathbf{x}_2, \nu_1, \nu_2) = \int f_1(\mathbf{y}_1 | \mathbf{x}_1, \nu_1) f_2(\mathbf{y}_2 | \mathbf{x}_2, \nu_2) g(\nu_1, \nu_2) d\nu_1 d\nu_2,$$

$$\simeq \frac{1}{S} \sum_{s=1}^{S} f_1(\mathbf{y}_1 | \mathbf{x}_1, \nu_1^{(s)}) f_2(\mathbf{y}_2 | \mathbf{x}_2, \nu_2^{(s)}), \qquad (4.25)$$

where the second line is a numerical approximation to the integral obtained by replacing ν_1, ν_2 by their simulated values and averaging over S pseudo-random draws from the assumed bivariate distribution. Maximizing this simulated likelihood function with respect to the unknown parameters is called Maximum Simulated Likelihood (MSL). Gourieroux and Monfort (1996) show that if S increases at a faster rate than the square root of the sample size, then MSL is asymptotically equivalent to maximum likelihood. Approaches for increasing the efficiency of numerical integration are available and will likely need to be employed if the joint distribution involves many parameters; see Train (2003).

The MSL estimation of a latent factor model has the theoretical advantage that it can be generalized to higher dimensions, although at additional and nontrivial computational cost. Like the copula approach it is based on marginals, which also is a potential advantage. Furthermore, Zimmer and Trivedi (2006) demonstrate that MSL produces similar results to copula models. However, in the present case the dependence structure will be restricted by the assumption of joint normality. This is an important consideration if the main focus is on estimating the dependence structure, whereas it is a lesser consideration if the main focus is on the regression function where the dependence parameter is treated as a nuisance parameter.

5

Conclusion

Copulas provide a potentially useful modeling toolkit in certain settings. Sklar's Theorem establishes that any multivariate distribution function with continuous margins has a unique copula representation. The result is the basis of the statement that "...much of the study of joint distributions can be reduced to the study of copulas," (Schweizer, 1991: 17). The result also indicates that copulas are a "recipe" for generating joint distributions by combining given marginal distributions according to a specified form of a copula function. Copulas are especially appealing because they capture dependence more broadly than the standard multivariate normal framework. A leading example is the case where the marginals belong to different families of distributions.

Inference about dependence can be implemented in a fully parametric or a partially parametric framework. However, as Hougaard (2000: 435) has observed, "...strictly speaking, copulas are not important from a statistical point of view. It is extremely rare that marginal distributions are known. Assuming the marginals are known is in almost all cases in conflict with reality. Copulas make sense, however, in a more broad perspective, first of all as part of the combined approach ... where the model is parameterized by means of the marginal distributions and

the copula. Second, they make sense for illustrating dependence. . .".
Consequently, modeling marginal distributions should be done with
care so that gross misspecification is avoided.

In certain empirical contexts, as we have illustrated, copulas are
computationally more attractive than the latent factor models to which
they are related. Latent factor models with errors generated by copulas
would appear to be a potentially attractive synthesis.

Several directions for future research on copula modeling could
be particularly helpful to practitioners. To deal with the standard
econometric issues of model misspecification, model diagnostics, and
model evaluation, diagnostic tests (e.g., score tests) based only on the
marginals would help narrow the set of copulas under consideration.
For example, one could test first for tail dependence of a specific type
and then narrow the range of copulas to be considered. More flexible
copula modeling would be possible if more flexible specifications for
higher dimensional copulas were to be developed.

References

Amemiya, T. (1973), 'Regression analysis when the dependent variable is truncated normal'. *Econometrica* **41**, 997–1016.

Amemiya, T. (1985), *Advanced Econometrics*. Cambridge: Harvard University Press.

Ané, T. and C. Kharoubi (2003), 'Dependence structure and risk measure'. *Journal of Business* **76**, 411–438.

Armstrong, M. (2003), 'Copula catalogue. Part 1: Bivariate Archimedean copulas'. Unpublished paper available at http://www.cerna.ensmp.fr.

Armstrong, M. and A. Galli (2002), 'Sequential nongaussian simulations using the FGM copula'. http://www.cerna.ensmp.fr/Documents/MA-AG-WPCopula.pdf.

Bouyé, E., V. Durrleman, A. Nikeghbali, G. Ribouletm, and T. Roncalli (2000), 'Copulas for finance: A reading guide and some applications'. Unpublished Manuscript, London: Financial Econometrics Research Centre, City University Business School.

Boyer, B. H., M. S. Gibson, and M. Loretan (1999), 'Pitfalls in tests for changes in correlations'. Federal Reserves Board, IFS Discussion Paper No 597R.

Brown, E. and H. Lankford (1992), 'Gifts of money and gifts of time: Estimating the effects of tax prices and available time'. *Journal of Public Economics* **47**, 321–341.

Cameron, A. C., T. Li, P. K. Trivedi, and D. M. Zimmer (2004), 'Modeling the differences in counted outcomes using bivariate copula models: With application to mismeasured counts'. *Econometrics Journal* **7**, 566–584.

Cameron, A. C. and P. K. Trivedi (1998), *Regression Analysis of Count Data*, Econometric Society Monographs 30. New York: Cambridge University Press.

Cameron, A. C., P. K. Trivedi, F. Milne, and J. Piggott (1988), 'A microeconomic model of the demand for health care and health insurance in Australia'. *Review of Economic Studies* **55**, 85–106.

Chambers, J. M., C. L. Mallows, and B. W. Stuck (1976), 'A method for simulating stable random variables'. *Journal of the American Statistical Association* **71**, 340–344.

Chen, X. and Y. Fan (2006), 'Estimation and model selection of semiparametric copula-based multivariate dynamic models under copula misspecification'. *Journal of Econometrics*.

Cherubini, U., E. Luciano, and W. Vecchiato (2004), *Copula Methods in Finance*. New York: John Wiley.

Chib, S. (1992), 'Bayes regression for the Tobit censored regression model'. *Journal of Econometrics* **51**, 79–99.

Chib, S. and R. Winkelmann (2001), 'Markov chain Monte Carlo analysis of correlated count data'. *Journal of Business and Economic Statistics* **19**, 428–435.

Clayton, D. G. (1978), 'A model for association in bivariate life tables and its application in epidemiological studies of familial tendency in chronic disease incidence'. *Biometrika* **65**, 141–151.

Clayton, D. G. and J. Cuzick (1985), 'Multivariate generalizations of the proporational hazards model'. *Journal of Royal Statistical Society Series B* **34**, 187–220.

Cont, R. (2001), 'Empirical proeprties of asset returns: Stylized facts and statistical issues'. *Quantitative Finance* **1**, 223–236.

Cook, R. D. and M. E. Johnson (1981), 'A family of distributions for modelling non-elliptically symmetric multivariate data'. *Journal of Royal Statistical Society B* **43**(2), 210–218.

de la Peña, V. H., R. Ibragimov, and S. Sharakhmetov (2003), 'Characterizations of joint distributions, copulas, information, dependence and decoupling, with applications to time series'. 2nd Erich L. Lehmann Symposium – Optimality, IMS Lecture Notes – Monograph Series, (J. Rojo, Ed.), In Press.

Deb, P., P. K. Trivedi, and P. Varangis (1996), 'Excess Co-movement in commodity prices reconsidered'. *Journal of Applied Econometrics* **11**, 275–291.

Denuit, M. and P. Lambert (2005), 'Constraints on concordance measures in bivariate discrete data'. *Journal of Multivariate Analysis* **93**, 40–57.

Devroye, L. (1986), *Non-Uniform Random Variate Generation.* New York: Springer-Verlag.

Drouet-Mari, D. and S. Kotz (2001), *Correlation and Dependence.* London: Imperial College Press.

Durbin, J. and A. S. Stuart (1951), 'Inversions and rank correlations'. *Journal of Royal Statistical Society Series B* **2**, 303–309.

Durrleman, V., A. Nikeghbali, and T. Roncalli (2000), 'How to get bounds for distribution convolution? A simulation study and an application to risk management'. GRO Credit Lyonnais, working paper.

Embrechts, P., A. McNeil, and D. Straumann (2002), 'Correlation and dependence in risk management: Properties and pitfalls'. In: M. A. H. Dempster (ed.): *Risk Management: Value at Risk and Beyond.* Cambridge: Cambridge University Press, pp. 176–223.

Fang, K.-T. and Y.-T. Zhang (1990), *Generalized Multivariate Analysis.* Berlin and New York: Springer-Verlag.

Frank, M. J. (1979), 'On the simultaneous associativity of F(x,y) and x+y - F(x,y)'. *Aequationes Math* **19**, 194–226.

Frees, E., J. Carriere, and E. Valdez (1996), 'Annuity valuation with dependent mortality'. *Journal of Risk and Insurance* **63**, 229–261.

Frees, E. W. and E. A. Valdez (1998), 'Understanding relationships using copulas'. *North American Actuarial Journal* **2**(1), 1–26.

Genest, C. and J. Mackay (1986), 'The joy of copulas: Bivariate distributions with uniform marginals'. *The American Statistician* **40**, 280–283.

Genest, C., Q. Molina, and R. Lallena (1995), 'De L'impossibilité de Constuire des lois a Marges Multidimensionnelles Données a Partir de Copules'. *Comptes Rendus de l'Académie des Sciences Serie I, Mathematique* **320**, 723–726.

Genest, C. and L. Rivest (1993), 'Statistical inference procedures for bivariate Archimedean copulas'. *Journal of the American Statistical Association* **88**(423), 1034–1043.

Genius, M. and E. Strazzera (2004), 'The copula approach to sample selection modelling: An application to the recreational value of forests'. Working paper, The Fondazione Eni Enrico Mattei.

Georges, P., A.-G. Lamy, A. Nicolas, G. Quibel, and T. Roncalli (2001), 'Multivariate survival modeling: A unified approach with copulas'. Unpublished paper, France: Groupe de Recherche Opérationnelle Crédit Lyonnais.

Gourieroux, C. and A. Monfort (1996), *Simulation Based Econometric Methods*. New York: Oxford University Press.

Greene, W. H. (1990), 'Multiple roots of the Tobit log-likelihood'. *Journal of Econometrics* **46**, 365–380.

Gumbel, E. J. (1960), 'Distributions des Valeurs Extremes en Plusieurs Dimensions'. *Publications de l'Institute de Statistíque de l'Université de Paris* **9**, 171–173.

Heckman, J. (1976), 'The common structure of statistical models of truncation, sample selection, and limited dependent variables and a simple estimator for such models'. *Annals of Economics and Social Measurement* **5**, 475–492.

Heckman, J. J. and B. E. Honoré (1989), 'The identifiability of the competing risks model'. *Biometrika* **76**, 325–330.

Heinen, A. and E. Rengifo (2003a), 'Comovements in trading activity: A multivariate autoregressive model of time series count data using copulas'. CORE Discussion Paper.

Heinen, A. and E. Rengifo (2003b), 'Multivariate modelling of time series count data: An autoregressive conditional Poisson model'. CORE Discussion Paper.

Hoeffding, W. (1940), 'Scale-invariant correlation theory'. In: N. I. Fisher and P. K. Sen (eds.): *The Collected Works of Wassily Hoeffding*. New York: Springer-Verlag, pp. 57–107.

Hoeffding, W. (1941), 'Scale-invariant correlation measures for discontinuous distributions'. In: N. I. Fisher and P. K. Sen (eds.): *The Collected Works of Wassily Hoeffding*. New York: Springer-Verlag, pp. 109–133.

Hougaard, P. (1986), 'A class of multivariate failure time distributions'. *Biometrika* **73**, 671–678.

Hougaard, P. (1987), 'Modeling multivariate survival'. *Scandinavian Journal of Statistics* **14**, 291–304.

Hougaard, P. (2000), *Analysis of Multivariate Survival Data*. New-York: Springer-Verlag.

Hougaard, P., B. Harvald, and N. V. Holm (1992), 'Measuring the similarities between the lifetimes of adult Danish twins born between 1881–1930'. *Journal of the American Statistical Association* **87**, 17–24.

Hu, L. (2004), 'Dependence patterns across financial markets: A mixed copula approach'. The Ohio State University, working paper.

Huang, H.-C. (1999), 'Estimation of the SUR Tobit model via the MCECM algorithm'. *Economics Letters* **64**, 25–30.

Huang, H.-C., F. A. Sloan, and K. W. Adamache (1987), 'Estimation of seemingly unrelated Tobit regressions via the EM algorithm'. *Journal of Business and Economic Statistics* **5**, 425–430.

Husler, J. and R. Reiss (1989), 'Maxima of normal random vectors: Between independence and complete dependence'. *Statistics and Probability Letters* **7**, 283–286.

Hutchinson, T. P. and C. D. Lai (1990), *Continuous Bivariate Distributions, Emphasising Applications*. Sydney, Australia: Rumsby.

Joe, H. (1990), 'Families of min-stable multivariate exponential and multivariate extreme value distributions'. *Statistics and Probability Letters* **9**, 75–81.

Joe, H. (1993), 'Parametric families of multivariate distributions with given margins'. *Journal of Multivariate Analysis* **46**, 262–282.

Joe, H. (1994), 'Multivariate extreme-value distributions with applications to environmental data'. *Canadian Journal of Statistics* **22**(1), 47–64.

Joe, H. (1997), *Multivariate Models and Dependence Concepts*. London: Chapman & Hall.

Junker, M. and A. May (2005), 'Measurement of aggregate risk with copulas'. *Econometrics Journal* **8**, 428–454.

Kamakura, W. A. and M. Wedel (2001), 'Exploratory Tobit factor analysis for multivariate censored data'. *Multivariate Behavioral Research* **36**, 53–82.

Kimeldorf, G. and A. R. Sampson (1975), 'Uniform representations of bivariate distributions'. *Communications in Statistics* **4**, 617–627.

Klugman, S. A. and R. Parsa (2000), 'Fitting bivariate loss distributions with copulas'. *Insurance: Mathematics and Economics* **24**, 139–148.

Lee, L. (1983), 'Generalized econometric models with selectivity'. *Econometrica* **51**, 507–512.

Li, D. X. (2000), 'On default correlation: A copula function approach'. *Journal of Fixed Income* **9**, 43–54.

Machado, J. A. F. and J. M. C. Santos Silva (2005), 'Quantiles for counts'. *Journal of the American Statistical Association* **100**, 1226–1237.

Marshall, A. (1996), 'Copulas, marginals, and joint distributions'. In: L. Ruschendorf, B. Schweizer, and M. D. Taylor (eds.): *Distributions with Fixed Marginals and Related Topics*. Hayward, CA: Institute of Mathematic Statistics, pp. 213–222.

Marshall, A. W. and I. Olkin (1967), 'A multivariate exponential distribution'. *Journal of the American Statistical Association* **62**, 30–44.

Marshall, A. W. and I. Olkin (1988), 'Families of multivariate distributions'. *Journal of the American Statistical Association* **83**, 834–841.

Marshall, A. W. and I. Olkin (1990), 'Multivariate distributions generated from mixtures of convolution and product families'. In: H. W. Block, A. R. Sampson, and T. H. Savits (eds.): *Topics in Statistical*

Dependence, Vol. 16 of *IMS Lecture Notes-Monograph Series*. pp. 371–393.

Meester, S. and J. MacKay (1994), 'A parametric model for cluster correlated categorical data'. *Biometrics* **50**, 954–963.

Meng, X. and D. B. Rubin (1996), 'Efficient methods for estimating and testing seemingly unrelated regressions in the presence of latent variables and missing observations'. In: D. A. Berry, K. M. Chaloner, and J. K. Geweke (eds.): *Bayesian Analysis in Statistics and Econometrics*. John Wiley & Sons, Inc, pp. 215–227.

Miller, D. J. and W. H. Liu (2002), 'On the recovery of joint distributions from limited information'. *Journal of Econometrics* **107**, 259–274.

Morgenstern, D. (1956), 'Einfache Beispiele Zweidimensionaler Verteilungen'. *Mitteilingsblatt fur Mathematische Statistik* **8**, 234–235.

Munkin, M. and P. K. Trivedi (1999), 'Simulated maximum likelihood estimation of multivariate mixed-poisson regression models, with application'. *Econometric Journal* **1**, 1–21.

Nelsen, R. B. (1991), 'Copulas and association'. In: G. Dall'Aglio, S. Kotz, and G. Salinetti (eds.): *Advances in Probability Distributions with Given Marginals*. Dordrecht: Kluwer Academic Publishers, pp. 31–74.

Nelsen, R. B. (2006), *An Introduction to Copulas*. 2nd edition. New York: Springer.

Oakes, D. (1982), 'A model for association in bivariate survival data'. *Journal of Royal Statistical Society B* **44**, 414–422.

Patton, A. (2005a), 'Modelling asymmetric exchange rate dependence'. *International Economic Review*. Forthcoming.

Patton, A. (2005b), 'Estimation of multivariate models for time series of possibly different lengths'. *Journal of Applied Econometrics*. forthcoming.

Pitt, M., D. Chan, and R. Kohn (2006), 'Efficient Bayesian inference for Gaussian copula regression'. *Biometrika* **93**, 537–554.

Prieger, J. (2002), 'A flexible parametric selection model for non-normal data with application to health care usage'. *Journal of Applied Econometrics* **17**, 367–392.

Prokhorov, A. and P. Schmidt (2006), 'Robustness, redundancy, and validity of copulas in likelihood models'. Working Paper, Michigan State University.

Schweizer, B. (1991), 'Thirty years of copulas'. In: G. Dall'Aglio, S. Kotz, and G. Salinetti (eds.): *Advances in Probability Distributions with Given Marginals: Beyond the Copulas*. The Netherlands: Kluwer Academic Publishers.

Schweizer, B. and A. Sklar (1983), *Probabilistic Metric Spaces*. New York: North Holland.

Schweizer, B. and E. F. Wolff (1981), 'On nonparametric measures of dependence for random variables'. *Annals of Statistics* **9**, 870–885.

Sklar, A. (1973), 'Random variables, joint distributions, and copulas'. *Kybernetica* **9**, 449–460.

Skrondal, A. and S. Rabe-Hesketh (2004), *Generalized Latent Variable Modeling: Multilevel, Longitudinal and Structural Equation Models*. Boca Raton, FL: Chapman & Hall/CRC.

Smith, M. (2003), 'Modeling selectivity using archimedean copulas'. *Econometrics Journal* **6**, 99–123.

Smith, M. (2005), 'Using copulas to model switching regimes with an application to child labour'. *Economic Record* **81**, S47–S57.

Song, P. X. (2000), 'Multivariate dispersion models generated from Gaussian copula'. *Scandinavian Journal of Statistics* **27**, 305–320.

Song, P. X. K., Y. Fan, and J. D. Kalbfleisch (2005), 'Maximization by parts in likelihood inference'. *Journal of the American Statistical Association* **100**, 1145–1158.

Stevens, W. L. (1950), 'Fiducial Limits of the parameter of a discontinuous distribution'. *Biometrika* **37**, 117–129.

Train, K. E. (2003), *Discrete Choice Methods with Simulation*. New York: Cambridge University Press.

Van Ophem, H. (1999), 'A general method to estimate correlated discrete random variables'. *Econometric Theory* **15**, 228–237.

Van Ophem, H. (2000), 'Modeling selectivity in count data models'. *Journal of Business and Economic Statistics* **18**, 503–511.

Vuong, Q. (1989), 'Likelihood ratio test for model selection and nonnested hypotheses'. *Econometrica* **57**, 307–333.

Wales, T. J. and A. D. Woodland (1983), 'Estimation of consumer demand systems with binding non-negativity constraints'. *Journal of Econometrics* **21**, 263–285.

Wang, W. (2003), 'Estimating the association parameter for copula models under dependent censoring'. *Journal of the Royal Statistical Society B* **65**, 257–273.

Zimmer, D. M. and P. K. Trivedi (2006), 'Using trivariate copulas to model sample selection and treatment effects: Application to family health care demand'. *Journal of Business and Economic Statistics* **24**, 63–76.

A

Copulas and Random Number Generation

Simulation is a useful tool for understanding and exhibiting dependence structures of joint distributions. According to Nelsen (2006: 40), "one of the primary applications of copulas is in simulation and Monte Carlo studies." Draws of pseudo-random variates from particular copulas can be displayed graphically, which allows one to visualize dependence properties such as tail dependence. Methods of drawing from copulas are also needed when conducting Monte Carlo experiments. This chapter presents selected techniques for drawing random variates from bivariate distributions and illustrates them with a few examples. In our experience, the appropriate method for drawing random variables depends upon which distribution is being considered; some methods are best suited for drawing variables from particular distributions. We do not claim that the methods outlined below are necessarily the "best" approaches for any given application. Rather, in our experience, the following approaches are straightforward to implement and provide accurate draws of random variates.

Random variates can be plotted to show dependence between variables. Many copula researchers rely on scatter plots to visualize differences between various copulas (Embrechts et al., 2002). Other researchers report pdf contour plots (Smith, 2003), which are presumably easier to interpret than three-dimensional pdf graphs. Nevertheless, some researchers report combinations of pdf contour plots and three-dimensional graphs (Ané and Kharoubi, 2003), while others report all three: scatter plots, contour graphs, and three-dimensional figures (Bouyé et al., 2000). All three techniques convey the same information, so whichever presentation one chooses is essentially a matter of preference. We use scatter plots for several reasons. First, scatter plots are easier to generate than pdf contour plots or three-dimensional figures and do not require complicated graphing software. Second, random draws used to create scatter plots are also useful for generating simulated data in Monte Carlo experiments. Third, scatter plots can be easily compared to plots of real life data to assist in choosing appropriate copula functions. Finally, we feel that interpretations are more straightforward for scatter plots than they are for pdf contour plots or three-dimensional figures.

A.1   Selected Illustrations

In this section, we sketch some algorithms for making pseudo-random draws from copulas. These algorithms can be viewed as adaptations of various general methods for simulating draws from multivariate distributions.

A.1.1   Conditional sampling

For many copulas, conditional sampling is a simple method of simulating random variates. The steps for drawing from a copula are:

- Draw u from standard uniform distribution.
- Set $y = F^{(-1)}(u)$ where $F^{(-1)}$ is any quasi-inverse of F.
- Use the copula to transform uniform variates. One such transformation method uses the conditional distribution of

U_2, given u_1.

$$c_{u_1}(u_2) = \Pr[U_2 \leq u_2 | U_1 \leq u_1]$$
$$= \lim_{\Delta u_1 \to 0} \frac{C(u_1 + \Delta u_1, u_2) - C(u_1, u_2)}{\Delta u_1}$$
$$= \frac{\partial}{\partial u_1} C(u_1, u_2).$$

By Theorem 2.2.7 in Nelsen (2006), a nondecreasing function $c_{u_1}(u_2)$ exists almost everywhere in the unit interval.[1]

In practice, conditional sampling is performed through the following steps:

- Draw two independent random variables (v_1, v_2) from $U(0,1)$.
- Set $u_1 = v_1$.
- Set $u_2 = C_2(u_2 | u_1 = v_1) = \partial C(u_1, u_2)/\partial u_1$.

Then the pair (u_1, u_2) are uniformly distributed variables drawn from the respective copula $C(u_1, u_2; \theta)$. This technique is best suited for drawing variates from the Clayton, Frank, and FGM copulas; see Armstrong and Galli (2002). The following equations show how this third step is implemented for these three different copulas (Table A.1).

A.1.2 Elliptical sampling

Methods for drawing from elliptical distributions, such as the bivariate normal and bivariate t-distribution, are well-established in statistics.

Table A.1 Selected conditional transforms for copula generation.

Copula	Conditional copula
Clayton	$u_2 = \left(v_1^{-\theta} \left(v_2^{-\theta/(\theta+1)} - 1 \right) + 1 \right)^{-1/\theta}$
Frank	$u_2 = -\frac{1}{\theta} \log \left(1 + \frac{v_2(1 - e^{-\theta})}{v_2(e^{-\theta v_1} - 1) - e^{-\theta v_1}} \right)$
FGM	$u_2 = 2v_2 / \left(\sqrt{B} - A \right)$
	$A = \theta(2u_1 - 1); B = [1 - \theta(2u_1 - 1)]^2 + 4\theta v_2 (2u_1 - 1)$

---

[1] See Example 2.20 in Nelsen (2006: 41–42) which gives the algorithm for drawing from $C(u_1, u_2) = u_1 u_2/(u_1 + u_2 - u_1 u_2)$.

These same methods are used to draw values from the Gaussian copula. The following algorithm generates random variables u_1 and u_2 from the Gaussian copula $C(u_1, u_2; \theta)$:

- Generate two independently distributed $N(0,1)$ variables v_1 and v_2.
- Set $y_1 = v_1$.
- Set $y_2 = v_1 \cdot \theta + v_2\sqrt{1 - \theta^2}$.
- Set $u_i = \Phi(y_i)$ for $i = 1, 2$ where Φ is the cumulative distribution function of the standard normal distribution.

Then the pair (u_1, u_2) are uniformly distributed variables drawn from the Gaussian copula $C(u_1, u_2; \theta)$.

A.1.3   Mixtures of powers simulation

To make draws from the Gumbel copula using conditional sampling, we need to calculate $C_2(u_2|v_1)$ which requires an iterative solution, which is computationally expensive for applications with many simulated draws. Marshall and Olkin (1988) suggest an alternative algorithm based on **mixtures of powers**. The following algorithm shows how the technique is used to generate draws from the Gumbel copula:

- Draw a random variable γ having Laplace transformation $\tau(t) = \exp(-t^{1/\theta})$. See below for additional detail.
- Draw two independent random variables (v_1, v_2) from $U(0,1)$.
- Set $u_i = \tau\left(-\gamma^{-1}\ln v_i\right)$ for $i = 1, 2$.

Then (u_1, u_2) are uniformly distributed variables drawn from the Gumbel copula.

However, to implement the first step we have to draw a random variable γ from a positive stable distribution $PS(\alpha, 1)$. This is accomplished using the following algorithm by Chambers et al. (1976).

- Draw a random variable η from $U(0, \pi)$.
- Draw a random variable w from the exponential distribution with mean equal to 1.

- Setting $\alpha = 1/\theta$, generate

$$z = \frac{\sin((1-\alpha)\eta)(\sin(\alpha\eta))^{\frac{\alpha}{1-\alpha}}}{\sin(\eta)^{\frac{1}{1-\alpha}}}.$$

- Set $\gamma = (z/w)^{(1-\alpha)/\alpha}$.

Then γ is a randomly draw variable from a $PS(\alpha,1)$ distribution.

A.1.4 Simulating discrete variables

Methods for drawing discrete variables depend upon which type of discrete variate is desired. We focus on simulating discrete Poisson variables using a method based on Devroye's technique of sequential search (Devroye, 1986). The algorithm is as follows:

- Draw correlated uniform random variables (u_1, u_2) from a particular copula using any of the methods discussed above.
- Set the Poisson mean $= \mu_1$ such that $\Pr(Y_1 = 0) = e^{-\mu_1}$.
- Set $Y_1 = 0$, $P_0 = e^{-\mu_1}$, $S = P_0$.
- If $u_1 < S$, then Y_1 remains equal to 0.
- If $u_1 > S$, then proceed sequentially as follows. While $u_1 > S$, replace (i) $Y_1 \leftarrow Y_1 + 1$, (ii) $P_0 \leftarrow \mu_1 P_0 / Y_1$, (iii) $S \leftarrow S + P_0$. This process continues until $u_1 < S$.

These steps produce a simulated variable Y_1 with Poisson distribution with mean λ_1. To obtain draws of the second Poisson variable Y_2, replace u_1 and μ_1 with u_2 and μ_2 and repeat the steps above. Then the pair (Y_1, Y_2) are jointly distributed Poisson variables with means μ_1 and μ_2.

LaVergne, TN USA
07 April 2010
178469LV00001B/83/A

9 781601 980205